Madama Butterfly

Madama Butterfly

GIACOMO PUCCINI

TEXT BY DANIEL S. BRINK

BLACK DOG
& LEVENTHAL
PUBLISHERS
NEW YORK

Published by
Black Dog & Leventhal Publishers, Inc.
151 West 19th Street
New York, NY 10011

Distributed by
Workman Publishing Company
708 Broadway
New York, NY 10003

Designed by Alleycat Design, Inc.

Series editor: Jessica MacMurray

Photo Research: Diana Gengora

Book manufactured in Singapore

ISBN: 1-57912-019-9

h g f e d

FOREWORD

Madama Butterfly is a tragic story of love, misunderstanding, cultural mismatching, honor and dishonor, all woven together. A seemingly simple tale about a young Japanese girl and her love for an American soldier who is careless with her devotion, *Butterfly* is brought to life—and eventually to her death—by Puccini's powerfully heartbreaking music. He touches on so many aspects of the human experience—overwhelming love, unbearable loss, rejection, motherhood, and clashing cultural ideals—with tenderness, honesty and poignance.

Explore the pages of this book: learn about the origins of the operas, the lives of the composers, and the world of opera singers and conductors. Listen to the complete opera on the two CD's included in the inside front and back covers of this book, while following along with the complete libretto. You will find both an English and an Italian version, complete with annotations by the author.

Enjoy this book and enjoy the music.

ABOUT THE AUTHOR

$\mathcal{D}$aniel S. Brink is the Artistic Advisor and Principal Coach/ Accompanist for the Colorado Opera Festival, Artistic Director for the Company Singers, a development program for young operatic hopefuls and Artistic Director/Conductor of the Colorado Springs Choral Society small ensemble, MOSIAC. Mr. Brink is a lecturer in Music and principal accompanist at The Colorado College, and has performed extensively in the United States and Europe. He is a highly regarded director, recitalist, teacher, adjudicator and writer.

ACKNOWLEDGEMENTS

I would like to thank Annette Megneys of the Colorado College Music Library and Jan Boothroyd, Executive Director of the Colorado Opera Festival for their invaluable assistance in researching this project. I would also like to thank my editor, Jessica MacMurray, whose influence afforded me the opportunity to write about these beloved works.

GIACOMO PUCCINI (1858-1924)
IN A PORTRAIT BY ARTURO RIETTI.

Madama Butterfly

At the beginning of the twentieth century, Giacomo Puccini had already established himself as the heir apparent to Giuseppe Verdi—the leading Italian opera composer for the better part of the 1800s. In keeping with the nineteenth-century ideal of the suffering artist, Puccini had had his share of struggles in achieving this standing.

Giacomo Puccini was born on December 22, 1858, in the small provincial capital of Lucca, in Tuscany. He was the seventh of eight children (six of whom were elder sisters) born to Michele and Albina-Magi Puccini. For five generations, Puccini men had studied at the conservatory in Naples. There they acquired the requisite skills to maintain the honored position of Maestro Di Capella Palatina at the Cathedral of San Martino in Lucca. The Puccini

family had manned this post since 1739, and it was expected that the young Giacomo would also assume the family's musical duties at the cathedral in due course.

However, it was not to be. In January of 1864, when Giacomo was five years old, his father died unexpectedly. It was decided that his widow's brother, Fortunato Magi, would assume the musical leadership at the Cathedral until the young Giacomo was old enough and sufficiently trained to take over his late father's position. Although his intention to follow in his father's footsteps was never realized, he would, in fact, become the last and most famous of the composing Puccinis—but in a far different artistic arena.

Giacomo's childhood was undistinguished. He did not do well in school and had the reputation of being lazy, expending his creative energies on various pranks, rather than on his studies.

NOËL EADIE AS BUTTERFLY, 1928.

He was a tall and handsome young man with a winning smile whose charm always kept him just out of the reach of real trouble. His initial musical studies were undertaken with his uncle, Fortunato Magi, whose severe and even abusive tutorial style engendered little love for the art in his student. Magi believed that Giacomo showed no particular talent in music and frequently despaired that the boy had no potential as a professional.

The great light in the early part of Puccini's life was his mother, whose unfailing belief in him would clear the path for all his early successes. After his graduation from the local seminary school, where he repeated his final year of study, his mother enrolled him at the Pacini Institute, Lucca's music conservatory. It was there, under the sympathetic tutelage of Carlo Angeloni, that Puccini's musical route began to come into focus. Angeloni had been a student of Puccini's father, Michele, and had since distinguished himself as a composer of opera and choral works. He befriended young Giacomo, engaging him not only in the classroom, where he introduced Puccini to the genius of Verdi's scores, but also as a hunting partner in the countryside surrounding Lucca. Angeloni instilled in him a fascination with and love for music that his stern uncle never could.

Puccini's skills began to flourish, and he was soon able to contribute to the fiscal stability of his mother's household by working as an organist in local churches. It was also during this time that the adolescent Puccini developed his unfortunate passion for cigarettes, a habit which would eventually lead to his premature death from throat cancer in 1924. Ever the prankster, it is said that Puccini stole pipes from the various organs on which he performed and sold them for scrap metal to support his smoking habit. He also earned money by playing in a small dance orchestra. By the age of sixteen, he had so distin-

copyright
A.Dupont

guished himself at the Pacini Institute that he received the first prize in 1875 for organ performance.

Early in 1876, Puccini had his first taste of professional opera at the Teatro Nuovo (now the Teatro Verdi) in Pisa. It was a production of Verdi's *Aïda,* which had enjoyed unparalleled success since its premiere in Cairo in 1871. Giacomo and two friends walked seven hours to Pisa and, lacking the funds to buy tickets, hid in the empty gallery of the theater for three hours awaiting the performance. Some years later, Puccini said of that performance, "When I heard *Aïda* in Pisa, I felt that a musical window had opened for me."

PUCCINI'S VISION FOR ACT 1, IN A PAINTING DATED 1904.

Madama Butterfly Atto I

Despite this small tribute to Verdi, Puccini's art is cut from a much different cloth. Indeed, the style of his operas owes much to Richard Wagner, whom Verdi reviled. The majority of Verdi's operas are written as a series of set numbers, in what had been the Italian tradition. In contrast, Puccini's operas are "through composed"—a continuous outpouring of melody unified by the use of musical motives which represent specific characters, emotions and situations. Puccini's ability to cleverly and subtly manipulate these motives is one of the factors which sets him above his contemporaries working in the same style.

After graduation from the Pacini Institute, it became clear that Puccini's musical ambitions deserved to reach beyond the confines of the artistic life of Lucca. It was decided that he would go to study at the Conservatory in Milan, the center of Italian musical life and the home of La Scala—Italy's greatest opera house. But the Puccini family was not financially able to accomplish this feat. Nonetheless, Giacomo's mother was determined to see her son's potential realized. She petitioned the queen for a scholarship, which was granted. Support was also secured from her late husband's cousin, Dr. Nicolai Ceru, who had become interested in Giacomo's progress in the latter part of his studies at the Institute. The young Puccini would attend the Milan Conservatory.

Puccini arrived in Milan in the fall of 1880. At twenty-two years of age, he was past the normal acceptance age by several years, but the excellence of his entrance exams assured him a place at the Conservatory. There, as at the Pacini Institute, he was befriended by a sympathetic mentor. Amilcare Ponchielli was a fine composer and professor whose opera, La Gioconda, set the direction for Italian opera in the latter part of the nineteenth century and remains in the repertoire today.

Puccini's three years at the Milan Conservatory were characterized by extreme financial hardship on the one hand and great artistic joy, development and discovery on the other. In late June of 1883, he completed his final examinations more than satisfactorily and began work on his final composition project, an orchestral work entitled *Capriccio Sinfonico*. It would have an obligatory first performance under the baton of a leading conductor from La Scala, and if successful, it would open doors for Puccini at Italy's leading publishing houses. *Capriccio Sinfonico* premiered on July 14, 1883, and won Puccini critical

YASUKO HAYASHI AS BUTTERFLY.

praise. He graduated from the Milan Conservatory with the Bronze Medal, the school's highest honor.

During the six years following his graduation, Puccini produced his first two operatic efforts, *Le Villi* and *Edgar,* both with librettos by Fernando Fontana. Le Villi enjoyed a modicum of success and served to establish Puccini with Giulio Ricordi, the leading publisher of Italian opera at the time. Ricordi was the great Verdi's publisher as well, and he saw Puccini as the rightful successor to Verdi. Puccini's second opera, *Edgar,* however, was a failure. Both

works showed the promise of great things to come, but they suffered from weak librettos not well suited to Puccini's specific talents.

Personal problems also plagued Puccini during this period. Not long after the premiere of *Le Villi*, Puccini's mother died. The loss was devastating to the young composer, coming as it did just when he was beginning to prove himself worthy of her unfailing belief in him. After his mother's death, Puccini's return to work was slow and fitful, and he would never fully recover from the loss.

Puccini's private life at this time was tumultuous. He had always had an eye for the ladies, and he became involved with Elvira Bonturi Gemignani, the wife of a prominent businessman in Lucca. Their affair caused her to leave her husband, taking her small daughter with her and leaving a younger son with her husband. Several months later, on December 23, 1886, Elvira bore Puccini's only child, Antonio. The people of Puccini's hometown were outraged, and he would never live there again. Elvira stayed with Puccini, eventually marrying him after the death of her husband, but the passion which brought them together would wane in the ensuing years. Puccini's entire adult life was punctuated by various sexual scandals—both real and imagined—which scuttled any hope of domestic bliss with Elvira.

It was not only in Puccini's personal life that a fascination with women held sway. Seven of his twelve operas are named for their heroines, and eight of his major female characters die, their tragic deaths invariably linked in some way to their unwavering love for a naive or unscrupulous man.

In 1889, following the failure of *Edgar* and under increased pressure from his publishers to see a return on their investment—they had been supporting

THE ROYAL OPERA HOUSE AT COVENT GARDEN, LONDON.

PUCCINI AT A REHEARSAL FOR MADAMA BUTTERFLY.

him since 1884—Puccini began making plans for his next opera, *Manon Lescaut.* This subject, based on a novel by Abbe Prevost, had already been successfully set by Jules Massenet, a fact that only seemed to fire Giacomo's desire to tackle it. Here the young composer began to trust his own dramatic instincts and doggedly hounded his librettists until he got what he wanted. As a result, the libretto of *Manon Lescaut* can be attributed to no fewer than seven poets, including Ruggiero Leoncavallo, Marco Praga, Giuseppe Giacosa and Luigi Illica (with whom Puccini would have a long and fruitful collaboration), as well as Puccini's publisher, Giulio Ricordi, and even Puccini himself!

Until the premiere of *Manon Lescaut* on February 1, 1893, there had been no clear successor to Verdi's Italian operatic throne. Leoncavallo had successfully produced his famous *I Pagliacci,* Pietro Mascagni had achieved renown for *Cavalleria Rusticana* and Alfredo Catalani's *La Wally* had been highly acclaimed. Now Puccini hoped to join their ranks, and both the composer and his publisher were nervous, but hopeful.

There hopefulness was rewarded. *Manon Lescaut* was a complete triumph, both with the public and with the critics. In fact, it would be the only completely unqualified success of Puccini's career. Now, not only Ricordi, but the press hailed Puccini as the successor to the esteemed Verdi. In only a few years, *Manon* was performed throughout Europe and in South America. Puccini's future was secure, and his financial struggles were forever ended.

The rest, as they say, is history. Exactly three years after the premiere of *Manon,* on February 1, 1896, *La Bohème,* with libretto by Illica and Giacosa, was unveiled. Based on Henri Murger's *La Vie de Bohème*, the story of the poverty-stricken young Parisian artists was not uniformly praised by critics, but it was enthusiastically embraced by the public and quickly became a mainstay of the operatic repertoire. On January 14, 1900, amid rumored bomb threats and various other intrigues, Puccini's *Tosca* premiered. Reviews found fault with the subject and libretto, but agreed on the quality of the music. And though the opening-night audience was not overwhelmingly appreciative, the opera continued to play to sold-out houses. The team of Puccini, Illica, Giacosa and Ricordi appeared to be unbeatable.

Puccini divided his time between traveling to oversee productions of his operas in the capitals of Europe and enjoying the sanctuary of his villa in the sleepy village of Torre del Lago. There he could indulge his passion for hunting and fishing and compose in peace and quiet. Puccini was feted wherever he went, and he spent the rest of his life alternately buoyed by the adulation of the public and subdued by his basically shy and unassuming nature.

The summer of 1900 found Puccini in London to oversee the Covent Garden premiere of *Tosca*. At the suggestion of friends, he attended a performance of *Madame Butterfly,* a one-act melodrama by the successful American playwright and producer, David Belasco. Belasco's play was based on a novella by an American writer-journalist, John Luther Long, which had appeared in *Century Magazine* in January 1898. Puccini was deeply moved by the tragic story of the little geisha, and despite the fact that he understood no English, he was able to follow the plot. He was especially taken with Cio-Cio-San's night-long vigil awaiting Pinkerton's return and with the scene's accompanying lighting effects. In the Belasco version, this particular scene was completely wordless, but lasted fourteen minutes.

When he saw Belasco's *Madame Butterfly*, Puccini had been seeking a source for his next opera for several months. The process of choosing a new subject was always a restless time for him, and he relentlessly drove his collaborators until a story was chosen and a libretto was in his hands. Since the failure of

SYLVIA SYDNEY AND CARY GRANT IN A 1933 MOVIE VERSION OF BUTTERFLY.

DAVID BELASCO,
AUTHOR OF THE
ORIGINAL MADAME
BUTTERFLY.

Edgar, Puccini had been very careful to choose plots and characters that touched and convinced him personally. He had already entertained several possible stories for his next opera and found them all wanting, but he saw in this exotic tale the qualities that would inspire him again.

Immediately following the play's performance, Puccini supposedly approached Belasco asking permission for the rights to set *Madame Butterfly* as an opera. Verbal permission was granted, although it took many months for the official permission to come through. In the meantime, Illica and Giacosa were able to acquire Long's story and translate it into Italian in order to begin work.

Puccini was excited about the project, and the creative process went smoothly compared to the heated deliberations characteristic of the development of previous works. But injury and illness delayed the completion of *Butterfly*. Puccini had a passion for cars; he loved their speed and was among the first Italian composers to own one. On a foggy evening in February 1903, he was returning home from Lucca with Elvira and their son, Tonio, when their chauffeur rounded a slippery curve and went off the road. The vehicle landed fifteen feet down an embankment. Elvira and Tonio were able to walk away from the accident, but the driver's thigh was broken, and Puccini was trapped under the car, unconscious and with a severe fracture of his right tibia. Fortunately, a doctor living nearby had heard the crash and came to Puccini's aid, taking the composer to his home for the night.

The leg didn't mend properly and had to be rebroken and reset. The healing process was inexplicably slow, and his doctors discovered that Puccini had diabetes. Bedridden and unable to work, the despondent composer wrote to Illica, "Farewell to everything, farewell to *Butterfly*, farewell to my life. How can

I endure the terrible summer months? What will I do? My God, this is enough to age a newborn child." But by June there were signs of improvement, and when the completed libretto was delivered, Puccini devised a way to sit at the piano and work.

Slowly regaining his strength, and happy to be at work again, Puccini completed the score on December 27, 1903. He wrote to a friend, "It's not bad. We'll see."

The premiere was set for February 14, 1904, at La Scala in Milan. Because of Puccini's unaccustomed confidence in the quality of the work, a veil of secrecy surrounded the rehearsal period, with no previews of the libretto in the press and none of the customary invitations to the final rehearsal for the local intelligentsia. The scores were not even allowed to leave the theatre, so the singers had to study their roles on site.

Originally conceived as a prologue and two acts, then as three acts—one of which was to take place at the American Consulate as in Long's story—Puccini decided finally to set the work in two acts. The first act was the wedding and lasted an hour; the second act began three years after Pinkerton's departure and lasted almost an hour and a half. Illica, Giacosa and Ricordi were certain that the public, accustomed to acts lasting no more than forty minutes, would not stand for scenes of this length. They suggested that the second act be divided in two at the close of the vigil. The composer, however, was adamant and would not consider the alteration.

Puccini was pleased with his cast, especially Rosina Storchio as Cio-Cio-San, to whom he wrote before the opening, "My good wishes are superfluous! So true, so delicate, so moving is your great art that the public must succumb to it! . . . Tonight then, with sure confidence and much affection, dear child!"

A PAINTING OF
BUTTERFLY DONE
IN 1904 FOR THE
OPERA'S PRE-
MIERE.

The stage was set for a triumphant premiere. Puccini was confident, the music and the singers were ready to thrill the public, and the critics were poised to be amazed. But, despite (or because of) all the anticipation, the premiere was one of the greatest disasters in operatic history. The audience, at first apathetic, soon became hostile. The performance was continually interrupted by laughter, shouts, catcalls, animal noises and accusations that Puccini had stolen from himself and from other composers. At one point, Storchio's kimono was caught by a breeze and billowed up causing someone to shout, "Butterfly's pregnant . . . Toscanini's baby!" (The soprano and Arturo Toscanini were embroiled in a rather well-publicized affair at the time.) With the final curtain, stony silence.

Although it was clear to the press and to many in attendance that the hostility was borne out of envy of Puccini's unparalleled standing, he was devastated. He withdrew the opera and returned the advance which he had been paid. The work was not completely flawed, but both the opera and Puccini had fallen victim to a well-organized attempt to sabotage his extraordinary career.

Within a week, Puccini, still convinced that *Butterfly* was his best work to date, began work with his librettists on revisions, which were surprisingly few. The wedding scene in the first act was tightened up, deleting unnecessary details; an intermission was added to the second act, as Puccini's collaborators had requested; Pinkerton's aria, *Addio, fiorito asil,* was added—this had been a bone of contention with Giacosa, whose lines were now restored; and the final encounter with Pinkerton's American wife, Kate, was reworked.

PUCCINI WITH HIS LIBRETTISTS, GIUSEPPE GIACOSA AND LUIGI ILLICA.

On May 28, 1904, the revised opera was given at the smaller provincial house at Brescia, although the house was again filled with critics and interested parties from Milan. It was a complete triumph, with thirty-two curtain calls and seven encores. Puccini's faith in his little Butterfly was vindicated, and the opera officially began its journey toward continuing international fame and success.

Puccini's faith in his work was well-founded. Though he was accused of rehashing ideas already heard in *La Bohème,* nothing could have been further from the truth. He had gone to great pains to incorporate oriental flavors into his score. A number of the melodies he used are authentic Japanese folk songs which he learned in interviews with the wife of the Japanese Ambassador to Italy and through other research. He also constructed original tunes based on the pentatonic scale—a five-note scale used extensively in Japanese music. Yet, these oriental colors never seem like self-conscious interpolations into the score. They are always fully integrated into Puccini's own style.

This score also marks Puccini's first extensive use of the whole-tone scale and the harmonies derived from it. This ambiguous sound is thought of as an "impressionistic" musical tool, most closely identified with the work of Claude Debussy, a French contemporary of Puccini's whom he greatly admired. In his next opera, *La Fanciulla del West* (The Girl of the Golden West), Puccini used this technique even more lavishly, having been exposed to Debussy's opera, *Pelleas et Melisande.*

Since the early days of his career, Puccini had always been lauded for his colorful orchestrations, and *Butterfly* represented his richest score to date. The

ARTURO TOSCANINI (1867-1957).

percussion section is employed liberally and includes the unusual sounds of Japanese bells and Japanese tam-tam or gong. As morning breaks following Butterfly's vigil awaiting Pinkerton's arrival, the score even requires bird calls. He also employs an unusual technique in the famous *Humming Chorus* heard during Butterfly's vigil, using voices as instruments, an innovation he would repeat in later scores.

In short, Puccini was not a composer willing to rest on his laurels. He constantly challenged himself to expand the palette of musical colors and textures from which he produced his art.

How is it that this opera survives while the story and play on which it is based have fallen into oblivion? At the turn of the twentieth century, the countries of the Far East had been open to the west for some forty years, and there was widespread interest among westerners in oriental culture. Eastern settings were popular in the Western theatre and in literature, but while the delicacy and balance of Eastern art was highly appreciated, the people of the Far East were perceived as backward. Western nations sought to "improve" the culture of the Far East with the infiltration of western, Christian ideals.

The condescending Western view of the Japanese people is all too clear in the work of Long and Belasco. Cho-Cho-San's (her name is spelled differently in the Belasco version) pidgin English is an embarrassing parody, not unlike the treatment of African-American speech in the popular Minstrel shows of the same era. These works would never hold the stage today.

Puccini's appreciation of, and perspective on, the international picture is debatable. Unlike Verdi, whose intricate plots frequently reflected some social or political injustice, Puccini chose to focus his art on the intimate setting of human emotions. While Pinkerton is certainly a cad to Puccini, he is at least partially redeemed by his remorseful acknowledgment of what his actions have caused. And Butterfly, while naive, is still afforded the dignity of beautiful and poetic Italian dialogue. Thus, Puccini's protagonists, regardless of their setting, are characters who are focused, essentially, on the human experience, and to whom the world will always relate.

The Story Of The Opera

ACT I

The curtain opens on a beautiful Japanese scene: a small, delicate Japanese house on a hill overlooking the harbor and city of Nagasaki. An American Naval Officer, Benjamin Franklin Pinkerton, is being given a tour of the house he is to rent with his new bride, Cio-Cio-San (who he has never seen), by Goro, the marriage broker. The young American is delighted with the movable walls and their functional flexibility, and he makes a point to ask the location of the bedroom.

With a clap of his hands, Goro summons the servants. Among them is Suzuki, Cio-Cio-San's longtime personal maid and confidante. She proceeds to recite a litany of compliments to her new American employer, but is interrupted by Pinkerton who inquires about the guest list for the wedding. Goro enumerates the many friends, relatives and officials who will be in attendance.

Sharpless, the American Consul, breathlessly enters after his climb up the hill. As Sharpless admires the house and the view, Pinkerton explains that he has leased the property for nine hundred ninety-nine years, an agreement which can be canceled in any month he chooses. To the opening phrase of "The Star Spangled Banner," Pinkerton rhapsodizes about the life of a young naval officer, going where he chooses, facing adventures of every sort, and having a love in every port. Sharpless comments about the irresponsibility of the young man's vision, but his opinion goes unnoticed. They toast to "America forever!"

Pinkerton asks Goro if his young bride is beautiful. Goro responds with poetic descriptions of the young geisha and then is suddenly sent away to see if she's coming.

Sharpless inquires as to whether Pinkerton's intentions in this marriage are honorable. Pinkerton replies that he is only living for the moment and, for the moment, he must possess Butterfly. Sharpless confesses that the girl had visited his office and that she seemed to take the marriage quite seriously. He warns the officer not to break her heart, but his warning goes unheeded, and Pinkerton proposes a toast to the happy day when he will have a real marriage to an American girl.

Suddenly, Goro reenters, and women's voices can be heard in the distance. Butterfly and her friends are about to arrive. As they climb the hill, the girls remark about the beauty of the sea and sky, and Butterfly's voice soars above them, declaring that in all the world there is no happier girl than she, for love

RENATA SCOTTO IN A 1986 PRODUCTION AT THE METROPOLITAN OPERA IN NEW YORK.

BUTTERFLY, WAITING
FOR PINKERTON'S
RETURN, SINGS OF
HER FRUSTRATION
AND LONELINESS,
ACT II.

is to greet her at the top of the hill. Upon their arrival, she asks her companions to bow to Pinkerton.

Pinkerton is charmed by Butterfly's innocence and beauty. Sharpless asks if she is from Nagasaki. Butterfly replies she is, and from a once wealthy family, but now they are poor and must work as geishas to keep the wolf from the door. The Americans are amused by her candor. When asked about her family, Butterfly replies that she has no siblings, only her poverty-stricken mother. Sharpless inquires about her father, and she curtly responds, "Dead." The gentlemen then engage in a guessing game regarding her age. She finally confesses that she is fifteen, rather old. The Americans respond in shocked delight—she is only a child.

Other guests are arriving, and Goro announces the presence of the Imperial Commissioner, the Registrar and Cio-Cio-San's family. The family members mill around, gossiping negatively about Pinkerton, Butterfly and the whole affair. Pinkerton, in turn, finds the family amusing. Goro tries to quiet them, and Sharpless comments how lucky Pinkerton is to have found such a lovely creature. But he warns Pinkerton again that Butterfly's love is in earnest and therefore he should be careful.

As the family goes into the garden, Pinkerton shows Butterfly the house. She takes the opportunity to show Pinkerton some of the things she has brought with her, asking his permission to keep them. She has brought some silk kerchiefs, a belt, a pipe, a mirror, a fan, and various other personal items. When Pinkerton reacts with amusement to a jar of makeup, she quickly discards it. She holds up a long narrow box, and Pinkerton asks her what it holds. She replies that it is something sacred, and he may see it when there are not so many people around. In an aside, Goro explains to Pinkerton that it is the knife the Mikado had sent to her father, with the order to kill himself, which he did. Butterfly has also brought her *Ottoke,* small statues representing the spirits of her ancestors.

Taking Pinkerton aside, Butterfly confides that early that morning she went to the Mission, and for love of him, had abandoned her religion to embrace his American God. She confesses that she would abandon family, friends—everything—for love of him.

Goro calls for silence, and the brief marriage ceremony takes place, involving only the reading and signing of a document. Congratulations are offered all around, and the officials and Sharpless prepare to leave. As he goes, Sharpless warns Pinkerton one last time to be prudent.

Pinkerton proposes a toast to their marriage, but as they are about to drink, the festive mood is interrupted by the arrival of Butterfly's uncle, the Bonze. In angry tones, he informs the guests that Butterfly had gone to the mission and betrayed her family and her religion, for which he reviles her. Pinkerton responds angrily, ordering him to leave. The Bonze and the family comply, but not before they vehemently renounce Butterfly. Their outraged cries continue as they leave.

Pinkerton tenderly turns to comfort Butterfly, saying that all the Bonzes in Japan are not worth one tear from her lovely eyes. She feels better and kisses his hand, saying she's been told it is a sign of great respect in his culture. They are interrupted by a voice from the house. Butterfly tells Pinkerton it is only Suzuki saying her evening prayers.

They observe that night is falling, and Suzuki is asked to close the house and bring Butterfly's robe. Butterfly goes in to change and comes out in the radiant white robe of a bride. Pinkerton is smitten. They join in a rapturous love duet, and Pinkerton asks her to confess her love. She declares her joy at their marriage, and in tender phrases she asks Pinkerton to love her only a little, as he would love a baby, purely and humbly. His ardor increases, but she is hesitant, having heard that in America, when butterflies are caught, they are impaled and imprisoned in a glass case. He admits that this is true, but that it is only done so the butterflies may not fly away. Gradually she succumbs to the lure of the night and his advances, and they go inside.

ACT II

Part 1

The curtain opens on Suzuki and Butterfly in a semi-darkened room of the house. It has been three years since Pinkerton's departure. Suzuki prays in a sorrowful monotone to the Japanese household gods. Butterfly, no longer the innocent girl, stands immobile and declares that the Japanese gods are fat and lazy. She is sure her American god would answer their prayers more quickly, but he probably doesn't know where they are.

Butterfly asks how long it will be before they run out of money and starve, waiting for her American husband's return. Suzuki shows her a few coins, saying that if Pinkerton doesn't return soon they will have nothing but trouble. Butterfly insists he will come. Suzuki is dubious. In an increasingly heated exchange, Butterfly tries to convince Suzuki of his return. He had promised, after all, to return when the robins nest. Butterfly insists Suzuki admit he will return. Suzuki finally does, but then breaks into sobs.

Butterfly's angry insistence abates, and in comforting tones she describes his return. One fine day, a ship will enter the harbor—his ship—and they will see him begin to climb the hill. She will not respond to his call at first, partly to tease him, partly so she won't die from joy and excitement at their first encounter. All this will come to pass, she assures Suzuki, and she will wait for him with certain faith.

Goro and Sharpless arrive, and Butterfly welcomes the American Consul to her "American" household with enthusiasm. She is the perfect hostess until Sharpless informs her that he has brought a letter from Pinkerton. This news only enhances her joy. She inquires as to the nesting habits of robins in America, whereupon she hears Goro laughing (he has remained outside) and sends him away. Sharpless feigns ignorance regarding the difference in nesting patterns between Japanese and American robins.

Butterfly tells him that Goro insists that she marry a wealthy local prince, Yamadori. She no sooner finishes, but Goro reenters, telling Sharpless that Butterfly is in dire straits because her family has disowned her. Suddenly, Yamadori enters in a flurry of princely grandeur to woo Butterfly. She greets him with polite amusement, but tells him that she is already married. Goro and Yamadori assert that her marriage to Pinkerton is at an end and that she has been abandoned. She responds dramatically that in America, wives are not so easily divorced. An American husband who tried to leave his wife would be dealt with by the courts. She concludes her speech offhandedly and sends Suzuki for tea. The suitor and his agent ask Sharpless to try to make Butterfly listen to reason: Her husband no longer wants her, but they've heard Pinkerton's ship is due.

Sharpless interrupts, telling them that Pinkerton doesn't want to see her, and he has been sent to deliver the bad news. Yamadori once again offers Butterfly his heart and hand, but she politely refuses, and she is left alone with Sharpless.

They sit together so that Sharpless can read Pinkerton's letter to her, but the reading is continually interrupted by her rhapsodic reflections upon hearing his words. Sharpless stops short when the bad news is about to be read, and asks her what she would do if Pinkerton were not to return. Butterfly is wounded by the suggestion. In halting phrases, she responds that she could go back to being a geisha, or better, she could die. Sharpless gently suggests she consider Yamadori's offer. Even more deeply wounded by this thought, Butterfly asks Suzuki to see Sharpless to the door. Apologetically, he turns to go, but turns back to her again when she suddenly feels faint.

In a defiant tone, Butterfly asks, "He forgot me?" She turns and leaves the room as a triumphant theme surges in the orchestra. She returns carrying the child who is the result of her marriage to Pinkerton, and she asks if he, too, will be forgotten. Sharpless, shocked, inquires if Pinkerton knows of the child's existence. She replies that he doesn't, but surely if he knew a son awaited him, he would return. Addressing the child, who is too young to understand, Butterfly marvels that Sharpless would send her into the streets again to entertain as a geisha, begging for the support of the public for her and her child. She reaffirms that she would rather die. Moved by her plight, Sharpless assures her that Pinkerton will be informed about his son. He asks the child's name, and Butterfly directs the child to tell Sharpless that his name is Sorrow, but upon his father's return, his name will be Joy. Sharpless departs.

PUCCINI, FOUR YEARS BEFORE HIS DEATH, IN A 1920 PORTRAIT.

BUTTERFLY, CONFIDENT THAT HER HUSBAND WILL
RETURN, DENIES YAMADORI'S PROPOSAL, ACT II.

A sharp cry is heard from Suzuki. She has found Goro lurking outside and has learned that he has been spreading the rumor that the child is illegitimate. In a rage, Butterfly grabs the knife with which her father committed *hara-kiri* and swoops toward Goro. As he narrowly escapes, Butterfly turns to the child and hysterically assures him of his father's return. Suddenly, a gunboat thunders in the harbor.

Butterfly and Suzuki take a small telescope from the table and rush to the terrace. Butterfly strains to identify the incoming ship. It is the *Abraham Lincoln*—Pinkerton's ship! Butterfly's faith in his return is vindicated. The women proceed to fill the house and its entrance with flowers to welcome Pinkerton. Butterfly then asks Suzuki's help in dressing herself for his arrival. Looking in the mirror, she notices that her long wait has aged her face, and she decides to mask the toll of her sorrow with a small application of color. She also colors the cheeks of her little son. Cutting three small holes in the paper wall of the little house, Butterfly, her son and her servant take their places to wait and watch for Pinkerton's arrival. Night falls to the accompaniment of the off-stage *Humming Chorus*. The child gradually falls asleep and Suzuki rests, but Butterfly steadfastly stares out at the city below.

ACT II

Part 2

As the curtain opens we hear sailors calling to one another in the harbor. Day is dawning and Butterfly has not moved. Suzuki rouses from her sleep and convinces Butterfly to take the child and get some rest, assuring her that she will awaken her when Pinkerton arrives.

No sooner have Butterfly and the child retired then there is a knock at the door. It is Sharpless and Pinkerton, who immediately silence Suzuki's excitement, telling her not to rouse Butterfly. Suzuki tells them of their preparations for Pinkerton's arrival and of Butterfly's all-night vigil. She then notices a woman in Victorian dress standing in the garden. She nervously inquires about the lady's identity, and Sharpless finally tells her it is Kate, Pinkerton's American wife. Suzuki bursts into sobs of despair. Sharpless explains that they arrived early to enlist her aid in asking Butterfly to give up the child to Pinkerton and Kate. A moving trio ensues in which Sharpless tries to persuade Suzuki to intercede for them with Butterfly, Pinkerton reflects on the flood of memories that surround him in the little house, and Suzuki reflects on the hopelessness of Butterfly's situation.

Pinkerton is overcome with remorse and says he must leave. Sharpless pointedly reminds him that he was warned of the potential for this disaster before his wedding. In an emotional outpouring, Pinkerton bids farewell to his flowered haven and the happiness he had known there. Admitting that he is the vile cause of all of Butterfly's sorrows, he flees the scene.

YASUKO HAYASHI
AS BUTTERFLY.

Suzuki then promises Kate she will tell Butterfly of Pinkerton's wish to take their son, but she demands that she must be allowed to break the news in private. At that moment we hear Butterfly call to Suzuki from the other room. Suzuki's efforts to keep Butterfly from entering are in vain—she knows Pinkerton has arrived! She searches the room excitedly, but he is nowhere to be found. She sees Sharpless, then notices Kate in the garden and asks who she is and what she wants. Sharpless replies that Kate is the innocent cause of all Butterfly's sorrows and asks forgiveness for her. Butterfly realizes the truth. She will be asked to surrender her son. After a moment of desperate disbelief, she resigns herself and says she will obey Pinkerton's wishes. Kate asks Butterfly if she will ever be able to forgive her. In a magnanimous gesture, Butterfly wishes Kate happiness and tells her that Pinkerton may return in half an hour to get the child. Sharpless and Kate depart.

Butterfly collapses, weeping. She tells Suzuki to close up the room—there is too much light and too much springtime. Suzuki complies. Butterfly asks where the child is. Suzuki tells her he is playing and offers to bring him to her, but Butterfly tells her to let him play and to go and be with him. Suzuki objects, but Butterfly sternly orders her to go, and she tearfully complies.

Alone, Butterfly kneels before the image of Buddha. She then takes the knife with which her father had killed himself, kisses it and reads the inscription on the blade aloud: "Let him die with honor who can no longer live with honor." She lifts the blade to plunge it into her throat, when suddenly Suzuki pushes the child into the room. He runs toward her with outstretched arms.

Butterfly drops the knife, embraces the child, and in a poignant aria bids farewell to her son, begging him to look well at her features and always to remember her. She then tells him to go and play. She hands him a doll and an

American flag, gently blindfolds him and faces him away from her. She takes up the knife, goes behind a screen and stabs herself. We hear the knife drop, and Butterfly begins to crawl from behind the screen to hold her child one last time. In the distance, we hear Pinkerton call her name, but as he and Sharpless arrive she falls dead beside her son. Pinkerton falls on his knees beside her lifeless body, and Sharpless, sobbing, embraces her orphaned child.

Madama Butterfly

GIACOMO PUCCINI 1858-1924

Madama Butterfly..Renata Scotto
Suzuki..Anna Di Stasio
Kate Pinkerton..Silvana Padoan
B. F. Pinkerton...Carlo Bergonzi
Sharpless..Rolando Panerai
Goro..Piero De Palma
Prince Yamadori...Giuseppe Morresi
Il Bonzo..Paolo Montarsolo
Il Commissario..Mario Rinaudo

Conducted by Sir John Barbirolli C. H.
Orchestra e Coro del Teatro dell'Opera di Roma
Chorus Master: Gianni Lazzari

The Artists

RENATA SCOTTO (Cio-Cio-San) was born in Savona, Italy. She began her vocal studies at age 14 as a mezzo-soprano, but after two years of study moved to Milan, where, under the guidance of Mercedes Llopart, she became a soprano. After winning a competition, Scotto was afforded the opportunity to make her debut in 1952 in her home town as the tragic Violetta in Verdi's *La Traviata*. In 1953 she repeated the role at Milan's Teatro Nuovo, and the following year, just barely in her twenties, she made her debut at La Scala. There, she sang the secondary role of Walter in Catalani's *La Wally*, but she soon left the famous house for the opportunity to sing leading roles in smaller provincial houses. Appearances in Rome and Venice soon followed, and by 1957 Scotto made her London debut as Mimi in Puccini's *La Bohème*. That same year, she got the "big break" that changed her professional life forever. On three days notice, she assumed the difficult role of Amina in Bellini's *La Sonnambula* at the Edinburgh Festival, replacing an ailing Maria Callas. Triumphant, Scotto returned to La Scala as a star, and her career was launched in all the major opera houses on both sides of the Atlantic and in Japan, where she was the first interpreter of the title role in Donizetti's *Lucia di Lammermoor*.

Scotto's American debut took place in 1960, again as Mimi, at the Chicago Lyric Opera. She debuted at New York's Metropolitan Opera in 1965 as Cio-Cio-San, the role heard here. Her early career included the bel canto roles of Lucia, Amina, Adina in Donizetti's *L'Elisir d'Amore,* and Bellini's *Norma,* as well as various Verdi and Puccini heroines. In the decades that followed she added to her repetoire such roles as Marguerite in Gounod's *Faust,* Berthe in Meyerbeer's *Le Prophete,* the heavier Verdi heroines, and verismo gems like the title role in Cilea's *Adriana Lecouvreur* and Maddalena in Giordano's *Andrea Chénier.* She was the first to sing all three heroines in Puccini's *Il Trittico* (three one-act operas) in one evening at the Met. Also at the Met, Scotto was the first performer ever to sing both Mimi and Musetta in *La Bohème* in a single season.

In recent years Scotto has moved into the German repertoire, singing the Marschalin in Strauss's *Der Rosenkavalier*

RENATA SCOTTO, 1986.

and a number of Wagner roles as well. In 1987, she made her directing debut with a production of *Madame Butterfly* at the Met, a production in which she, among others, also sang the title role. She now divides her time between singing, directing and concert work.

Scotto, with over twenty-five complete opera recordings to her credit, has always been known for her vocal beauty and agility and her unfailing dramatic instincts. She is the quintessential singing actress, and this recording finds her at the height of her powers. This *Butterfly* is the first of two complete recordings she did of the work, and she portrays the geisha's innocence and tender charm with unequaled perception and clarity.

CARLO BERGONZI (Lieutenant Benjamin Franklin Pinkerton) was born in Polisene, Italy—near Parma—in 1924. His initial studies were undertaken at the Boito Conservatory in Parma, but were interrupted by World War II, during which he was, for a time, a prisoner of the Nazis. After the war, he resumed his studies and made his debut in 1948 as a baritone in the role of Figaro in Rossini's *Il Barbiere di Siviglia* at Lecce. After a period of study, he debuted as a tenor in 1951 at Bari in the title role of Giordano's *Andrea Chénier.*

Bergonzi's La Scala debut took place in 1953 when he created the title role in Napoli's *Mas'Aniello,* and he continued to appear there until the early 1970s. He made his London debut at the Stoll Theatre in 1953 as Don Alvaro in Verdi's *La Forza del Destino,* and he repeated the role at his Covent Garden debut in 1962. He appeared at Covent Garden regularly until 1985. His final role there was as Edgardo in Donizetti's *Lucia di Lammermoor.*

American audiences first heard Bergonzi in 1955, when he debuted at the Chicago Lyric Opera in a double bill, singing Luigi in Puccini's *Il Tabarro* and

Turiddu in Mascagni's *Cavalleria Rusticana* in the same evening. In 1956, he debuted at the Metropolitan Opera as Radames in Verdi's *Aïda*. He sang at the Met for over thirty years, making his final appearance there in 1988 in the role of Rodolpho in Verdi's *Luisa Miller*.

Bergonzi had a beautiful lyrico-spinto voice and was prized for his seamless line and his capacity to sing soft phrases with ease and control, These talents stood him in good stead with the lighter Italian repertoire, including Alfredo in Verdi's *La Traviata* and Nemorino in Donizetti's *L'Elisir d'Amore*. Yet his voice had the power to soar over the orchestral texture, making his portrayals of the heavier repertoire, such as Verdi's Radames, equally attractive. His favorite role was that of Riccardo in Verdi's *Un Ballo in Maschera*.

In recent years Begonzi has made a series of farewell performances at the various houses graced by his talents through his 45-year career. He appeared in concert singing Neopolitan songs with The Opera Orchestra of New York as recently as April 1996. Today he makes occasional concert appearances, but spends much of his time at the Inn he owns and runs called *I Due Foscari* in Verdi's hometown of Busseto, Italy.

Bergonzi recorded over twenty complete operas, most of which are Verdi roles, but he recorded Pinkerton twice, first with Renata Tebaldi under Tullio Serafin in 1958, then in the recording heard here in 1966. At forty-two years of age, he portrays the American officer with a youthful vigor and an idealistic naivete that makes it difficult to paint him as a complete villain. This recording affords the listener an opportunity to hear Bergonzi at his very best.

ROLANDO PANERAI (Sharpless) was born in the small town of Campi Bisenzio, near Florence. He pursued his vocal studies in Florence and Milan and made his debut in 1946 in Florence as Enrico Ashton in Donizetti's *Lucia di Lammermoor*. Over the following two years he appeared regularly in Naples, where he had debuted as Pharaoh in Rossini's *Mose in Egitto,* and in 1951 he made his La Scala debut as the High Priest in Saint-Saën's *Samson et Dalila*. He appeared there regularly for a number of years, singing such diverse roles as Apollo in Gluck's *Alceste* and the husband in Menotti's comedy, *Amelia al Ballo*. In 1957 he sang the title role in the Italian premiere of Hindemith's *Mathis der Maler* at La Scala, and in 1962 he created the title role in Turchi's *Il buono soldat Svejk* there.

Panerai's international career began in 1955 when he created the role of Ruprecht in Prokofiev's *The Flaming Angel* in Aix-en-Provence. There he also portrayed Mozart's Figaro. He debuted in Salzburg in 1957 as Ford in Verdi's *Falstaff,* and his American debut was with the San Francisco Opera in 1958, where he sang both the Rossini and Mozart Figaros and Marcello in Puccini's *La Bohème.* His career has included all the major houses in Italy, Great Britain, France, Germany and the United States, including the Metropolitan in New York. He remains active today, emphasizing two of his latest specialties: the title roles in Verdi's *Falstaff* and Puccini's *Gianni Schicchi.*

Panerai's extensive discography includes over twenty complete operas, ranging from Mozart to Wagner in the German repertoire and from Rossini to Puccini in the Italian repertoire. This is his only recording of Sharpless, but it is one of his most effective audio portrayals. Known for his dark, vibrant sound and superb acting, Panerai's Sharpless is characterized by a warmth and beauty of tone and a tenderness of delivery. At the same time, it is never weak or ineffectual, as Sharpless is so often portrayed. Panerai contributes fully to what is a dream cast for this subtle and intricate opera.

SIR JOHN BARBIROLLI (1899-1970).

SIR JOHN BARBIROLLI (the conductor) was born in London in 1899 of Italian-French descent. He was a scholarship student at Trinity College of Music and the Royal Academy of Music, and at age seventeen, he became the youngest member of the Queen's Hall Orchestra. Barbirolli's first conducting experiences were with an all-volunteer orchestra while serving in the army. His work there led to an invitation in 1928 to conduct the British National Opera Company on tour. From 1929 to 1933 he served as guest conductor with Covent Garden, conducting their international and English seasons. In 1934 he conducted at the Sadler's Wells Opera Company, returning to Covent Garden in 1937.

What appeared to be a career focused in opera took a turn when Barbirolli accepted the musical leadership of the New York Philharmonic. Later he conducted the Halle Orchestra in Germany. He returned to opera only intermittently for the remainder of his career, most notably as guest conductor at Covent Garden for three seasons, between 1951 and 1954. Toward the end of his life he recorded this *Madame Butterfly* and Verdi's *Otello,* and conducted Verdi's *Aïda* in Rome in 1969.

Barbirolli was knighted in 1949, made Companion of Honour in 1969 and died in London in 1970. He recorded only the two complete operas mentioned above, but he left an extensive discography of the orchestral repertoire which is uniformly admired. He was especially fond of late romantic literature, and his skill is apparent in this recording. Puccini's lush orchestrations and soaring vocal lines frequently persuade conductors to take slower tempi, much to the dismay of many a singer and to Puccini himself, who frequently complained of lugubrious tempi in the performances of his operas. By contrast, Barbirolli here achieves an ideal balance of movement and restraint, demonstrating a thorough understanding of Puccini and the little geisha he immortalized.

The Libretto

Act 1

disc no. 1/track 1 The act opens with a vigorous motive beginning in the violins, then taken up in turn by the violas, cellos and basses n fugal style. Then Puccini introduces a sprightly little oriental theme **(00:31)**, after which the curtain opens and the winds take up the first theme again. Both of these motives are used throughout the opera.

A hill near Nagasaki. A Japanese house, with terraced garden. At back, below, the harbour and the city. Goro is showing the house to Pinkerton, who goes from one surprise to another.

PINKERTON
E soffitto...e pareti...

GORO
Vanno e vengono a prova
a norma che vi giova
nello stesso locale
alternar nuovi aspetti ai consueti.

PINKERTON
Il nido nuziale
dov'è?

PINKERTON
And ceiling and walls...

GORO
Go back and forth at will,
so that you can enjoy
from the same spot
different views to the usual ones.

PINKERTON
Where is
the nuptial nest?

GORO
Qui, o là...secondo...

PINKERTON
Anch'esso a doppio fondo!
La sala?

GORO*(mostrando la terrazza)*
Ecco!

PINKERTON
All'aperto?

GORO
Un fianco scorre...

PINKERTON
Capisco! Capisco!
Un altro...

GORO
scivola!

PINKERTON
È la dimora frivola...

GORO
Salda come una torre,
da terra fino al tetto.

PINKERTON
È una casa a soffietto.

GORO

GORO
Here, or there...depending...

PINKERTON
It has false ends,, too!
And the living room?

GORO *(indicating the terrace)*
There it is!

PINKERTON
In the open air?

GORO
One side slides along...

PINKERTON
I understand!
Another one...

GORO
...glides along!

PINKERTON
And this ridiculous little place...

GORO
Solid as a tower,
from floor to ceiling.

PINKERTON
...is a concertina house.

GORO

(claps his hands and two men and a woman enter and kneel before Pinkerton.)

Questa è la cameriera
che della vostra sposa
fu già serva amorosa.
Il cuoco. Il servitor. Sono confusi
del grande onore.

PINKERTON
I nomi?

GORO
"Miss Nuvola leggera."
"Raggio di sol nascente."
"Esala aromi."

SUZUKI
Sorride Vostro Onore?
Il riso è frutto e fiore.
Disse il savio Ocunama:
"Dei crucci la trama
smaglia il sorriso.
Schiude alla perla il guscio,
apre all'uom l'uscio
del Paradiso.
Profumo degli dei...
fontana della vita..."
Disse il savio Ocunama:
"Dei crucci la trama smaglia il sorriso."

This is the maid
who was your bride's
faithful servant before.
The cook. The manservant. They are
embarrassed by the great honour.

PINKERTON
Their names?

GORO
"Miss Light Cloud."
"Ray of the Rising Sun."
"The Aromatic One."

SUZUKI
Your Honour is smiling?
Laughter is fruit and flower.
The wise Ocunama has said:
"A smile breaks through
a web of trouble.
It opens the shell for the pearl,
to man it opens the gates
of Paradise.
Perfume of the gods...
fountain of life..."
The wise Ocunama has said:
"A smile breaks through a web of troubles."

(Goro realizes that Pinkerton is bored. He claps his hands. The three servants run back into the house.)

PINKERTON
A chiacchiere costei
mi par cosmopolita.
Che guardi?

GORO
Se non giunge ancor la sposa.

PINKERTON
By her chattering
she seems just like all woman the world
over. What are you looking at?

GORO
To see if the bride's coming yet.

PINKERTON
Tutto è pronto?

GORO
Ogni cosa.

PINKERTON
Gran perla di sensale!

GORO
Qui verran:
l'Ufficiale del Registro,
I parenti, il vostro Console,
la fidanzata.
Qui si firma l'atto
e il matrimonio è fatto.

PINKERTON
E son molti i parenti?

GORO
La suocera, la nonna,
lo zio Bonzo (che non
ci degnerà di sua presenza)
e cugini, e le cugine!
Mettiam fra gli ascendenti
ed i collaterali un due dozzine.
Quanto alla discendenza...
provvederanno assai
Vostra Grazia e la bella Butterfly.

PINKERTON
Gran perla di sensale!

VOCE DI SHARPLESS
E suda e arrampica!
Sbuffa, inciampica!

PINKERTON
Is everything ready?

GORO
Everything.

PINKERTON
Priceless pearl of a marriage-broker!

GORO
The Registrar,
the relations,
your Consul and the bride
will all come here.
You'll sign the documents here,
and you'll be married.

PINKERTON
And are there many relations?

GORO
The mother-in-law, the grandmother,
her uncle the Bonze (who won't
honour us with his presence),
and her male and female cousins...
Let's say, with ancestors
and contemporaries, about two dozen.
As for descendants...
Your Grace and the pretty Butterfly
will take good care of that.

PINKERTON
You priceless pearl of a marriage-broker!

VOICE OF SHARPLESS
You sweat and climb,
puff and stumble!

GORO
Il Consol sale.

SHARPLESS (*apparendo sbuffando*)
Ah! quei ciottoli
mi hanno sfiaccato!

PINKERTON
Bene arrivato!

GORO
Bene arrivato!

SHARPLESS
Ouff!

PINKERTON
Presto, Goro -
qualche ristoro.

SHARPLESS
Alto.

PINKERTON
Ma bello.

SHARPLESS
Nagasaki, il mare, il porto...

PINKERTON
...e una casetta
che obbedisce a bacchetta.

SHARPLESS
Vostra?

GORO
The Consul's coming up.

SHARPLESS (*appearing, out of breath*)
Those stones
have reduced me to a jelly!

PINKERTON
Welcome!

GORO
Welcome!

SHARPLESS
Uff!

PINKERTON
Quick, Goro,
some refreshments.

SHARPLESS
It's high up, here!

PINKERTON
But, it's beautiful!

SHARPLESS
Nagasaki, the sea, the harbour...

PINKERTON
And a little house
that works by magic.

SHARPLESS
Is it yours?

PINKERTON

La comperai per novecento
novantanove anni,
con facoltà, ogni mese,
di rescindere i patti.
Sono in questo paese
elastici del par,
case e contratti.

PINKERTON

I've bought it for nine hundred
and ninety-nine years,
with the right, every month,
to cancel the agreement.
In this country
houses and contracts
are equally elastic.

SHARPLESS

E l'uomo esperto ne profitta.

SHARPLESS

And the clever man makes the most of it.

PINKERTON

Certo.

PINKERTON

Certainly.

(Goro hurries from the house, followed by two servants bearing glasses, bottles, plates, cutlery and two wicker chairs. They lay two places at a little table, and return to the house.)

disc. no. 1/track 3   *Dovunque al mondo,* Pinkerton's ode to American world dominance, appropriately opens with a quote from "The Star Spangled Banner".

Dovunque al mondo
lo Yankee vagabondo
si gode e traffica
sprezzando rischi.
Affonda l'àncora
alla ventura...

Everywhere in the world
the roving Yankee
takes his pleasure and his profit,
indifferent to all risks.
He drops anchor
at random...

(He breaks off to offer a drink to Sharpless.)

Milk-punch, o wisky?
Affonda l'àncora
alla ventura
finché una raffica scompigli
nave e ormeggi, alberatura...

Milk punch or whisky?
...He drops anchor
at random
till a sudden squall wrecks
the ship, hawsers rigging and all...

La vita ei non appaga
se non fa suo tesor
i fiori d'ogni plaga...

SHARPLESS
È un facile vangelo...

PINKERTON
d'ogni bella gli amor.

SHARPLESS
...è un facile vangelo
che fa la vita vaga
ma che intristisce il cor.

PINKERTON
Vinto si tuffa,
la sorte riacciuffa.
Il suo talento
fa in ogni dove.
Così mi sposo
all'uso giapponese
per novecento
novantanove anni. Salvo
a prosciogliermi ogni mese.

SHARPLESS
È un facile vangelo.

PINKERTON
"America for ever!"

SHARPLESS
"America for ever!"
Ed è bella la sposa?

He's not satisfied with life
unless he makes his own
the flowers of every shore...

SHARPLESS
It's an easy-going creed.

PINKERTON
...the love of every pretty girl.

SHARPLESS
...an easy-going creed
that makes life delightful
but saddens the heart.

PINKERTON
If beaten,
he tries his luck again.
He follows his bent
wherever he may be.
So I'm marrying
in Japanese fashion
for nine hundred and
ninety-nine years. With the right
to be freed every month!

SHARPLESS
It's an easy-going creed.

PINKERTON
"America for ever!"

SHARPLESS
"America for ever!"
And is the bride pretty?

GORO (*udendo, si avanza.*)
Una ghirlanda di fiori freschi,
una stella dai raggi d'oro.
E per nulla: sol cento yen.
Se Vostra Grazia mi comanda
ce n'ho un assortimento...

PINKERTON
Va, conducila Goro.

SHARPLESS
Quale smania vi prende!
Sareste addirittura
cotto?

PINKERTON
Non so! non so! Dipende
dal grado di cottura!
Amore o grillo -
dir non saprei.
Certo costei m'ha colle ingenue
arti invescato.
Lieve qual tenue vetro soffiato
alla statura, al portamento
sembra figura da paravento.
Ma dal suo lucido fondo di lacca
come con subito moto
si stacca; qual farfalletta
svolazza e posa
con tal grazietta silenziosa,
che di rincorrerla
furor m'assale -
se pure infrangerne
dovessi l'ale.

GORO (*overhearing, comes forward.*)
A garland of fresh flowers,
a star with golden rays...
And for next to nothing: only a hundred
yen. If your Grace wishes
I have a good selection.

PINKERTON
Go and fetch her, Goro.

SHARPLESS
What madness has got hold of you!
Are you completely
infatuated?

PINKERTON
I don't know! It depends
on the degree of infatuation!
Love or passing fancy -
I couldn't say.
She's certainly bewitched me
with her innocent arts.
Delicate and fragile as blown glass,
in stature, in bearing
she resembles some figure on a painted
screen, but as, from her background of
glossy lacquer, with a sudden movement
she frees herself; like a butterfly
she flutters and settles
with such quiet grace
that a madness seizes me
to pursue her,
even though I might
damage her wings.

SHARPLESS

Ier l'altro, il Consolato
sen' venne a visitar!
Io non la vidi,
ma l'udii parlar.
Di sua voce il mistero
l'anima mi colpì.
Certo quando è sincer
l'amor parla così.
Sarebbe gran peccato
le lievi ali strappar
e desolar forse un credulo cor.
Quella divina mite vocina
non dovrebbe dar note di dolor.

PINKERTON

Console mio garbato,
quietatevi! si sa:
la vostra età è di flebile umor.
Non c'è gran male
s'io vo' quell'ale
drizzare ai dolci voli dell'amor!
Whisky?

SHARPLESS

Un'altro bicchiere.
Bevo alla vostra famiglia lontana.

PINKERTON

E al giorno in cui mi sposerò
con vere nozze
a una vera sposa americana.

GORO (riappare correndo)
Ecco! Son giunte
al sommo del pendìo.
Già del femmineo sciame

SHARPLESS

The day before yesterday she came
to visit the Consulate.
I didn't see her myself
but I heard her speak.
The mystery of her voice
touched me to the heart.
True love surely
speaks like that.
It would be a great sin
to strip off those delicate wings
and perhaps plunge a trusting heart into
despair. That heavenly, meek, pretty, little
voice shouldn't utter a note of sadness!

PINKERTON

My dear Consul,
don't worry! It's usual
at your age to take a pessimistic view.
There's no great harm done
if I want those wings
to be spread in love's tender flight!
Whisky?

SHARPLESS

Another little glassful.
Here's to your family at home.

PINKERTON

And to the day when I shall get married
in real earnest
to a real American bride.

GORO (re-enters at a run)
Here they come! They've reached
the top of the hill.
You can already hear the swarm

qual di vento in fogliame
s'ode il brusìo.

of women rustling like
leaves in the wind!

disc no. 1/track 5 *O quanto cielo, quanto mar.* Butterfly's entrance begins with shimmering high strings, then as she climbs the hill to meet her husband, the harmonies climb through several modulations. When Puccini finished this part, early in the creative process, he wrote to a friend, "I am pleased with it"--and rightfully so.

VOCE DI RAGAZZE Ah! ah! Quanto cielo! Quanto mar!	**GIRLS' VOICES** Ah! Ah! What an expanse of sky! What an expanse of sea!
VOCE DI BUTTERFLY Ancora un passo or via.	**VOICE OF BUTTERFLY** Just one more step now...
VOCE DI RAGAZZE Come sei tarda.	**GIRLS' VOICES** How slow you are!
VOCE DI BUTTERFLY Aspetta.	**VOICE OF BUTTERFLY** Wait.
VOCI DI RAGAZZE Ecco la vetta. Guarda, guarda quanti fior!	**GIRLS' VOICES** Here we are at the summit! Look, just look at all the flowers!
VOCE DI BUTTERFLY Spira sul mare e sulla terra un primaveril soffio giocondo.	**VOICE OF BUTTERFLY** Over land and sea there floats a joyous breath of spring.
SHARPLESS O allegro cinquettar di gioventù.	**SHARPLESS** Oh, the gay chatter of youth!
VOCE DI BUTTERFLY Io sono la fanciulla più lieta del Giappone,	**VOICE OF BUTTERFLY** I am the happiest girl in Japan,

anzi del mondo.
Amiche, son venuta
al richiamo d'amor...
D'amor venni alle soglie
ove s'accoglie il bene
di chi vive e di chi muor.

or rather, in the whole world.
Friends, I have come
at the call of love...
I have come to the portals of love
where is gathered the happiness
of all who live and die.

VOCI DI RAGAZZE
Gioia a te sia, dolce amica,
ma pria di varcar
la soglia che t'attira
volgiti e mira
quanto cielo, quanti fiori,
quanto mar; mira
le cose tutte che ti son sì care.

GIRLS' VOICES
Joy to you, sweet friend,
but before crossing
the threshold which draws you,
turn and look at
the things which you hold dear,
look at all that sky,
all those flowers and all that sea!

BUTTERFLY
Siam giunte.

BUTTERFLY
We have arrived.

(She sees the group of men and recognises Pinkerton. She closes her parasol smartly, and points Pinkerton out to her friends.)

B. F. Pinkerton. Giù.

B. F. Pinkerton. Down.

LE AMICHE
Giù.

GIRL FRIENDS
Down.

diasc no. 1/track 6 The bride and groom exchange pleasantries. When asked about her father, she responds "Dead," and we first hear the motive connected with the dagger **(02:55)** that took his life and will also, in the end, take Butterfly's.

BUTTERFLY
Gran ventura.

BUTTERFLY
Good luck attend you.

LE AMICHE
Riverenza.

GIRL FRIENDS
Our respects.

PINKERTON
È un po' dura
la scalata?

PINKERTON
The climb is
rather difficult?

BUTTERFLY
A una sposa costumata
più penosa è l'impazienza.

BUTTERFLY
To a court bride
impatience is more trying.

PINKERTON
Molto raro complimento.

PINKERTON
A very rare complement.

BUTTERFLY
Dei più belli ancor ne so.

BUTTERFLY
I know some even prettier ones.

PINKERTON
Dei gioielli!

PINKERTON
Real gems!

BUTTERFLY
Se vi è caro sul momento...

BUTTERFLY
If you like, this very instant...

PINKERTON
Grazie...no.

PINKERTON
Thank you...no.

SHARPLESS
Miss Butterfly...Bel nome,
vi sta a meraviglia.
Siete di Nagasaki?

SHARPLESS
Miss Butterfly. A pretty name -
it suits you to perfection.
Do you come from Nagasaki?

BUTTERFLY
Signor, sì. Di famiglia
assai prospera un tempo.

BUTTERFLY
Yes, sir. From a family
which at one time was quite well-to-do.

(to her friends)

Verità?

Isn't that so?

LE AMICHE
Verità.

BUTTERFLY
Nessuno si confessa mai
nato in povertà.
Non c'è vagabondo
che a sentirlo non sia
di gran prosapia. Eppur
conobbi la ricchezza.
Ma il turbine rovescia
le quercie più robuste
e abbiam fatto la ghescia
per sostentarci.

(to her friends)

Vero?

LE AMICHE
Vero!

BUTTERFLY
Non lo nascondo,
né m'adonto.
Ridete? Perché?
Cose del mondo...

PINKERTON
Con quel fare di bambola
quando parla m'infiamma.

SHARPLESS
Ed avete sorelle?

BUTTERFLY
No, signore. Ho la mamma.

GIRL FRIENDS
It is!

BUTTERFLY
No one ever admits
he was born in poverty.
There's not a beggar
who, to hear him, doesn't
come of high lineage. All the same,
I have known riches.
But storms uproot
the sturdiest oaks...
and we became geishas
to support ourselves.

That's so, isn't it?

GIRL FRIENDS
It is!

BUTTERFLY
I don't hide it,
neither do I feel hard done by.
Why do you laugh?
It's the way of the world.

PINKERTON
With those childlike ways,
when she talks she sets my blood on fire.

SHARPLESS
And have you any sisters?

BUTTERFLY
No, sir. I have my mother.

GORO
Una nobile dama.

BUTTERFLY
Ma senza farle torto,
povera molto anch'essa.

SHARPLESS
E vostro padre?

BUTTERFLY *(bruscamente)*
Morto.

SHARPLESS
Quant'anni avete?

BUTTERFLY
Indovinate.

SHARPLESS
Dieci.

BUTTERFLY
Crescete.

SHARPLESS
Venti.

BUTTERFLY
Calate.
Quindici netti, netti.
Sono vecchia diggià.

SHARPLESS
Quindici anni.

GORO
A noble lady.

BUTTERFLY
But without wronging her,
very poor, too.

SHARPLESS
And your father?

BUTTERFLY *(abruptly)*
Dead.

SHARPLESS
How old are you?

BUTTERFLY
Guess.

SHARPLESS
Ten.

BUTTERFLY
Make it more.

SHARPLESS
Twenty.

BUTTERFLY
Make it less.
Just exactly fifteen;
I'm already old.

SHARPLESS
Fifteen!

PINKERTON
Quindici anni!

SHARPLESS
L'età dei giuochi...

PINKERTON
E dei confetti.

GORO
L'Imperial Commissario,
l'Ufficiale del Registro,
i congiunti.

PINKERTON
Fate presto.

PINKERTON
Fifteen!

SHARPLESS
The age for games...

PINKERTON
...and wedding cake.

GORO
The Imperial Commissioner,
the Registrar,
the bride's family.

PINKERTON
Get on with it quickly.

(Goro runs into the house. Pinkerton talks apart to the Consul.)

Che burletta la sfilata
della nuova parentela!

CUGINI E PARENTI
Bello non è, in verità.
Bello non è.

BUTTERFLY
Bello è così
che non si può sognar di più.

MADRE ED AMICHE
Mi pare un re!
Vale un Perù!

CUGINA *(a Butterfly)*
Goro l'offrì pur anco a me,
ma s'ebbe un no!

What a farce, this parade
of my new relations,

COUSIN AND RELATIONS
He's not handsome, truly.
He's not handsome.

BUTTERFLY
He's so handsome
one just couldn't imagine anything better!

MOTHER AND FRIENDS
He seems like a king to me.
He's worth a fortune.

COUSIN *(to Butterfly)*
Goro offered him to me too,
but he has got no for an answer!

BUTTERFLY
Sì, giusto tu!

PARENTI (a Butterfly)
La sua beltà già disfiori.
Divorzierà.

CUGINA E **PARENTI**
Spero di sì.

LO ZIO YAKUSIDÉ
Vino ce n'è?
Guardiamo un po'.
Ne vidi già
color di thé e chermisì.

GORO
Per carità, tacete un po'!
Sch! Sch! Sch!

SHARPLESS
O amico fortunato!
O fortunato Pinkerton,
che in sorte v'è toccato
un fior pur or sbocciato.

PINKERTON
Sì, è vero, è un fiore, un fiore!
L'esotico suo odore
m'ha il cervello sconvolto.

CUGINA E **PARENTI**
Ei l'offrì pur anco a me,
ma risposi non lo vo'!

MADRE ED **AMICHE**
Egli è bel, mi pare un re!

BUTTERFLY
Of course, you would!

RELATIONS (to cousin)
Her looks have already faded.
He'll divorce her.

COUSIN AND **RELATIONS**
I hope so.

UNCLE YAKUSIDE
Is there any wine here?
Let's have a look.
I've just seen some the colour of tea,
and some red!

GORO
For goodness sake, keep quiet!
Sh! Sh! Sh!

SHARPLESS
My lucky young friend!
Lucky Pinkerton,
on whom Fate has bestowed
this newly opened flower!

PINKERTON
Yes, it's true, she's a flower, a flower!
Her exotic fragrance
has turned my head.

COUSIN AND **RELATIONS**
He offered him to me too,
but I answered I don't want him!

MOTHER AND **FRIENDS**
He's too handsome, he seems like a king to

Non avrei risposto no,
non direi mai no!

SHARPLESS
Non più bella e d'assai fanciulla
io vidi mai di questa Butterfly!
E se a voi sembran scede
il patto e la sua fede...

CUGINA ᴇ PARENTI
Senza tanto ricercar
io ne trovo dei miglior
e gli dirò un bel no.

MADRE ᴇᴅ AMICHE
No, mie care, non mi par,
è davvero un gran signor,
nè gli direi di no!

BUTTERFLY
Badate, attenti a me!

PINKERTON
Sì, è vero, è un fiore, un fiore,
e in fede mia l'ho colto!

SHARPLESS
Badate! Ella ci crede!

BUTTERFLY
Mamma, vien qua.
Badate a me:
attenti, orsù,
uno, due, tre,
e tutti giù.

me! I wouldn't have answered no,
I would never have said no!

SHARPLESS
No lovelier girl have I ever seen
than this Butterfly.
And if you don't take this contract
and her trust seriously...

COUSIN ᴀɴᴅ RELATIONS
Without looking too hard
I've found better,
and I shall roundly tell him no!

MOTHER ᴀɴᴅ FRIENDS
No, my dears, I didn't think so,
he's a real gentleman,
and I would not say no!

BUTTERFLY
Attention, listen to me.

PINKERTON
Yes, it's true, she's a flower, a flower,
and, upon my honour, I've plucked her!

SHARPLESS
...Beware! She believes in them!

BUTTERFLY
Mother, come here.
Listen to me:
attention, come now,
one, two, three,
and everybody down.

(They all bow low in front of Pinkerton and Sharpless. Pinkerton takes Butterfly's hand.)

disc no. 1/track 8   As Butterfly shows her few belongings to Pinkerton, Puccini uses a Japanese melody familiar to most Americans, "Sakura" **(01:10)**. Again, we hear the dagger theme **(02:04)** when Goro explains her father's suicide to Pinkerton.

PINKERTON
Vieni, amor mio!
Ti piace la casetta?

PINKERTON
Come, my love,
do you like our little house?

BUTTERFLY
Signor B. F. Pinkerton, perdono...
Io vorrei...pochi oggetti da donna...

BUTTERFLY
Mr. B. F. Pinkerton, excuse me...
I would like..a few woman's possessions...

PINKERTON
Dove sono?

PINKERTON
Where are they?

BUTTERFLY
Sono qui...vi dispiace?

BUTTERFLY
They're here...you don't mind?

(She produces various small objects from the capacious sleeves of her kimono.)

PINKERTON
O perché mai, mia bella Butterfly?

PINKERTON
Why ever should I, my pretty Butterfly?

BUTTERFLY
Fazzoletti. La pipa.
Una cintura. Un piccolo fermaglio.
Uno specchio. Un ventaglio.

BUTTERFLY
Handkerchiefs. Pipe.
A sash. A little clasp.
A mirror. A fan.

PINKERTON
Quel barattolo?

PINKERTON
What's that pot?

BUTTERFLY
Un vaso di tintura.

PINKERTON
Ohibò.

BUTTERFLY
Vi spiace?

(She throws it away.)

Via.

PINKERTON
E quello?

BUTTERFLY
Cosa sacra e mia.

PINKERTON
E non si può vedere?

BUTTERFLY
C'è troppa gente.
Perdonate.

GORO *(sottovoce a Pinkerton)*
È un presente del Mikado
a suo padre...coll'invito...

(He imitates the gesture of hara-kiri.)

PINKERTON
E...suo padre?

GORO
Ha obbedito.

BUTTERFLY
A jar of rouge.

PINKERTON
Oh dear!

BUTTERFLY
Don't you like it?

A way with it!

PINKERTON
And that?

BUTTERFLY
My most sacred possession.

PINKERTON
And mayn't one see it?

BUTTERFLY
There are too many people.
Forgive me.

GORO *(whispering to Pinkerton)*
It's a present from the Mikado
to her father...inviting him to...

PINKERTON
And her father?

GORO
Obeyed.

BUTTERFLY

BUTTERFLY

(taking some statuettes from her sleeve)

Gli Ottokè.

My Ottoke.

PINKERTON
Quei pupazzi? Avete detto?

PINKERTON
These puppets? You said?

BUTTERFLY
Son l'anime degli avi.

BUTTERFLY
They are the spirits of my ancestors.

PINKERTON
Ah! il mio rispetto.

PINKERTON
Oh! My respects.

BUTTERFLY
Ieri son salita tutta sola
in segreto alla Missione.
Colla nuova mia vita
posso adottare nuova religione.
Lo zio Bonzo nol sa,
né i miei lo sanno.
Io seguo il mio destino
 e piena d'umiltà
al Dio del signor Pinkerton
m'inchino.
È mio destino;
nella stessa chiesetta
in ginocchio con voi
pregherò lo stesso Dio.
E per farvi contento potrò forse
obliar la gente mia.
Amore mio!

BUTTERFLY
Yesterday I went, alone
and in secret, to the Mission.
With my new life
I can adopt a new religion.
My uncle, the Bonze, doesn't know,
neither do my people.
I follow my destiny
and, filled with humility,
I kneel before
Mr. Pinkerton's God.
It is my fate.
In the same little church,
beside you on my knees,
I will pray to the same God,
and to please you I may perhaps be able
to forget my own people.
My dearest love!

GORO
Tutti zitti!

GORO
Quiet, everybody!

IL COMMISSARIO
È concesso al nominato
Benjamin Franklin Pinkerton,
Luogotenente della cannoniera "Lincoln",
marina degli Stati Uniti,
America del Nord,
ed alla damigella Butterfly,
del quartiere d'Omara, Nagasaki,
d'unirsi in matrimonio,
per dritto il primo
della propria volontà,
ed ella per consenso dei parenti
qui testimoni all'atto...

GORO (con cerimonia)
Lo sposo.
Poi la sposa.
E tutto è fatto.

LE AMICHE
Madama Butterfly.

BUTTERFLY
Madama B. F. Pinkerton.

IL COMMISSARIO
Auguri molti.

PINKERTON
I miei ringraziamenti.

IL COMMISSARIO
Il Signor Console scende?

SHARPLESS
L'accompagno.

COMMISSIONER
It is permitted to the herein named
Benjamin Franklin Pinkerton,
Lieutenant in the warship Lincoln,
United States Navy,
North America,
and to Miss Butterfly
of the Omara district of Nagasaki,
to be united in matrimony,
the first by right
of his own wish
and she by consent of her relations
here witness to the contract.

GORO (with ceremony)
The bridegroom.
Then the bride.
And everything's concluded.

FRIENDS
Madam Butterfly!

BUTTERFLY
Madam B. F. Pinkerton.

COMMISSIONER
My best wishes.

PINKERTON
Many thanks.

COMMISSIONER
Are you going, sir?

SHARPLESS
I'll go along with you.

(to Pinkerton)

Ci vedrem domani.	See you tomorrow.

PINKERTON
A meraviglia.

PINKERTON
Capital.

UFFICIALE DEL REGISTRO
Posterità.

OFFICIAL REGISTRAR
May you have many descendants.

PINKERTON
Mi proverò.

PINKERTON
I'll try.

SHARPLESS *(partendo, a Pinkerton)*
Giudizio!

SHARPLESS *(going, to Pinkerton)*
Have a care!

(Sharpless, the Rigstrar and the Commissioner leave.)

PINKERTON *(a parte)*
Ed eccoci in famiglia.
Sbrighiamoci al più presto
in modo onesto.

PINKERTON*(to himself)*
And here we are in the family circle!
Let's get rid of all these people
as soon as we decently can.

(He raises his glass.)

Hip! Hip!

Hip! Hip!

PARENTI
O Kami! O Kami!

RELATIONS
O Kami! O Kami!

PINKERTON
Beviamo ai novissimi legami.

PINKERTON
Let's drink to the new ties.

(Suddenly a terrifying character appears. It is the Bonze, who comes forward in a rage; holding his hand out towards Butterfly, he threatens her.)

IL BONZO
Cio-Cio-San! Abominazione!

BUTTERFLY E PARENTI
Lo zio bonzo!

GORO
Un corno al guastafeste!
Chi ci leva d'intorno
le persone moleste?

IL BONZO
Cio-Cio-San! Che hai tu fatto
alla Missione?

TUTTI
Rispondi, Cio-Cio-San!

PINKERTON
Che mi strilla quel matto?

IL BONZO
Rispondi, che hai tu fatto?
Come, hai tu gli occhi asciutti?
Son dunque questi i frutti?
Ci ha rinnegato tutti.

TUTTI
Hou! Cio-Cio-San!

IL BONZO
Rinnegato vi dico...
il culto antico.

TUTTI
Hou! Cio-Cio-San!

BONZE
Cho-Cho-San! Abomination!

BUTTERFLY AND RELATIONS
Our uncle the Bonze!

GORO
Confound the spoilsport!
Who will rid us
of such nuisances?

BONZE
Cho-Cho-San! What were you up to
at the Mission?

ALL
Answer, Cho-Cho-San!

PINKERTON
What's that madman shouting about?

BONZE
Answer, what were you about?
What, can your eyes be dry!
So then, these are the fruits?
She has renounced us all.

ALL
Oh, Cho-Cho-San!

BONZE
I tell you she has renounced
our ancient faith.

ALL
Oh! Cho-Cho-San!

IL BONZO
Kami sarundasico!
All'anima tua guasta
qual supplizio sovrasta!

PINKERTON
Ehi, dico, basta, basta!

IL BONZO
Venite tutti.
Andiamo!
Ci hai rinnegato e noi
ti rinneghiamo!

PINKERTON
Sbarazzate all'istante.
In casa mia niente baccano
e niente bonzeria.

TUTTI (*partendo*)
Hou! Cio-Cio-San! Kami sarundasico.
Hou! Cio-Cio-San! Ti rinneghiamo!

PINKERTON
Bimba, bimba, non piangere
per gracchiar di ranocchi.

PARENTI (*lontani*)
Hou! Cio-Cio-San!

BUTTERFLY
Urlano ancor!

PINKERTON
Tutta la tua tribù
e i Bonzi tutti del Giappon
non valgono il pianto

BONZE
Kami sarundasico!
What torments
threaten your lost soul!

PINKERTON
Hey, that's enough, I say!

BONZE
Come, everybody!
Let us go!
You have renounced us and we
renounce you!

PINKERTON
Get out of here at once.
I'll have no shindy in my house
and none of this bonzing!

ALL (*leaving*)
Oh! Cho-Cho-San! Kami sarundasico!
Oh! Cho-Cho-San! We renounce you!

PINKERTON
Dear child, don't cry
over that croaking of frogs.

RELATIONS (*far off*)
Oh! Cho-Cho-San!

BUTTERFLY
They're still howling!

PINKERTON
The whole tribe of them
and all the bonzes in Japan
aren't worth a tear

di quegli occhi cari e belli.

BUTTERFLY
Davver? non piango più.
E quasi del ripudio
non mi duole
per le vostre parole
che mi suonan così dolci nel cor.

(She kisses his hand.)

PINKERTON
Che fai? La man?

BUTTERFLY
M'han detto che laggiù
fra la gente costumata
è questo il segno
del maggior rispetto.

SUZUKI *(dentro la casa)*
E Izaghi ed Izanami sarundasico,
e Kami, e Izaghi,
ed Izanami sarundasico, e Kami.

PINKERTON
Chi brontola lassù?

BUTTERFLY
È Suzuki che fa
la sua preghiera seral.

from your sweet, pretty eyes!

BUTTERFLY
Really? Then I won't cry any more.
And I scarcely mind
their repudiation
because of your words
which echo so sweetly in my heart.

PINKERTON
What are you doing? My hand?

BUTTERFLY
I've been told that over there
among well-bred people
it's a sign
of the greatest respect.

SUZUKI *(from inside the house)*
Izaghi, Izanami sarundasico,
Kami, Izaghi,
Izanami sarundasico, Kami.

PINKERTON
Who's that muttering in there?

BUTTERFLY
It's Suzuki saying
her evening prayers.

disc no. 1/track 11 *Vieni la sera.* Here begins one of the most famous love duets in all opera.
The music surges with Pinkerton's passion until at last he possesses Butterfly.

PINKERTON
Viene la sera.

BUTTERFLY
E l'ombra e la quiete.

PINKERTON
E sei qui sola.

BUTTERFLY
Sola e rinnegata!
Rinnegata...e felice!

PINKERTON

(claps; the servants run out.)

A voi, chiudete.

BUTTERFLY
Sì, sì, noi tutti soli...
E fuori il mondo...

PINKERTON
E il Bonzo furibondo!

BUTTERFLY
Suzuki, le mie vesti.

PINKERTON
Night is falling.

BUTTERFLY
And darkness and peace.

PINKERTON
And you are here alone.

BUTTERFLY
Alone and renounced!
Renounced and happy!

PINKERTON

Come here and close up the house.

BUTTERFLY
Yes, yes, we are all alone...
and the world shut outside...

PINKERTON
And the furious Bonze.

BUTTERFLY
Suzuki, my clothes.

(Suzuki goes to a chest and gives Butterfly her night clothes.)

SUZUKI
Buona notte.

BUTTERFLY
Quest'obi pomposa
di scioglier mi tarda...

SUZUKI
Good night.

BUTTERFLY
I long to take off
this ceremonial sash,

Si vesta la sposa
di puro candor.
Tra moti sommessi
sorride e mi guarda.
Celarmi potessi!
Ne ho tanto rossor!
E ancor l'irata voce
mi maledice...
Butterfly rinnegata,
rinnegata...e felice.

PINKERTON
Con moti di scoiattolo,
i nodi allenta e scioglie!
Pensar che quel giocattolo
è mia moglie! Mia moglie!
Ma tal grazia dispiega
ch'io mi struggo
per la febbre
d'un subito desìo.

let the bride be dressed
in pure white.
Whispering to himself
he smiles and watches me.
If I could only hide!
It makes me blush so!
And still the angry voice
is cursing me...
Butterfly renounced,
renounced... and happy.

PINKERTON
With squirrel-like movements
she shakes the knots loose and undoes
them!
To think that this little toy
is my wife! My wife!
But she displays such grace
that I am consumed
by a fever
of sudden desire!

(Pinkerton approaches Butterfly, who has finished dressing.)

Bimba dagli occhi pieni di malia
ora sei tutta mia.
Sei tutta vestita di giglio.
Mi piace la treccia tua bruna
fra candidi veli.

BUTTERFLY
Somiglio la dea della luna,
la piccola dea della luna
che scende la notte
dal ponte del ciel.

Dear child, with eyes full of witchery,
now you are all mine.
You're dressed all in lily-white.
I love your dark tresses
amid the white of your veils.

BUTTERFLY
I am like the moon-goddess,
the little goddess of the moon,
who comes down at night
from the bridge of heaven.

PINKERTON
E affascina i cuori...

BUTTERFLY
E li prende, e li avvolge
in un bianco mantel.
E via se li reca
negli alti reami.

PINKERTON
Ma intanto finor non m'hai detto,
ancor non m'hai detto che m'ami.
Le sa quella dea le parole
che appagan gli ardenti desir?

BUTTERFLY
Le sa. Forse dirle non vuole
per tema d'averne a morir,
per tema d'averne a morir!

PINKERTON
Stolta paura,
l'amor non uccide,
ma dà vita, e sorride
per gioie celestiali
come ora fa
nei tuoi lunghi occhi ovali.

PINKERTON
And captivates all hearts...

BUTTERFLY
...and takes them and folds them
in a white cloak.
And carries them away
to the higher regions.

PINKERTON
But meanwhile, you haven't told me yet,
you haven't told me you love me.
Does that goddess know the words
that satisfy burning desire?

BUTTERFLY
She does. Maybe she's unwilling
to say them for fear of dying of it,
for fear of dying of it!

PINKERTON
Foolish fear -
love does not kill,
but gives life and smiles
for heavenly joy,
as it does now
in your almond eyes.

disc no. 1/track 13 *Vegliatemi bene.* "Love me well," Butterfly says to the gentle accompaniment of a solo violin. This melody is repeated several times, modulating upward with increasing instrumentation and tension. At last she is ready to succumb, and we hear again the music of her entrance **(04:20)**, slowly climbing in passion just as she had slowly climbed the hill.

BUTTERFLY

Adesso voi siete per me
l'occhio del firmamento.
E mi piaceste dal primo momento
che vi ho veduto.
Siete alto, forte.
Ridete con modi sì palesi!
E dite cose
che mai non intesi.
Or son contenta. Or son contenta.
Vogliatemi bene, un bene piccolino,
un bene da bambino
quale a me si conviene.
Noi siamo gente avvezza
alle piccole cose,
umili e silenziose,
ad una tenerezza
sfiorante e pur profonda
come il ciel, come l'onda del mare.

PINKERTON

Dammi ch'io baci
le tue mani care,
mia Butterfly!
Come t'han ben nomata
tenue farfalla...

BUTTERFLY

Dicon ch'oltre mare
se cade in man dell'uom
ogni farfalla d'uno spillo
è trafitta
ed in tavola infitta!

PINKERTON

Un po' di vero c'è:
e tu lo sai perché?

BUTTERFLY

For me you are now
the eye of heaven.
And I liked you from the first moment
I set eyes on you.
You are tall and strong.
You laugh out so heartily.
And you say things
I've never heard in my life before.
I'm happy now, so happy.
Love me with a little love,
a child-like love,
the kind that suits me.
Love me, please...
We are a people used to small,
modest, quiet things,
to a tenderness gently caressing,
yet vast as the sky
and as the waves of the sea.

PINKERTON

Give me your dear hands
and let me kiss them!
My Butterfly!
How aptly you were named,
fragile butterfly!

BUTTERFLY

They say that overseas
if it should fall into the hands of man
a butterfly is stuck through
with a pin
and fixed to a board!

PINKERTON

There's some truth in that;
and do you know why?

Perché non fugga più.
Io t'ho ghermita...
Ti serro palpitante.
Sei mia.

BUTTERFLY
Sì, per la vita.

PINKERTON
Vieni, vieni...
Via dall'anima in pena
l'angoscia paurosa.
È notte serena! Guarda:
dorme ogni cosa!
Sei mia! Ah! vien!

BUTTERFLY
Ah! dolce notte! quante stelle!
Non le vidi mai sì belle!
Trema, brilla ogni favilla
col baglior d'una pupilla.
Oh! quanti occhi fisi, attenti,
d'ogni parte a riguardar!
pei firmamenti, via pei lidi,
via pel mare...ride il ciel!
Ah! dolce notte!
Tutto estatico d'amor,
ride il ciel!

So that it shouldn't fly away again.
I've caught you...
Quivering, I press you to me.
You're mine.

BUTTERFLY
Yes, for life.

PINKERTON
Come along, come...
Cast all sad fears
out of your heart!
The night is clear! See,
all things sleep!
You are mine! Oh, come!

BUTTERFLY
Oh, lovely night! What a lot of stars!
Never have I seen them so beautiful!
Every spark twinkles and shines
with the brilliance of an eye.
Oh! What a lot of eyes fixed and staring,
looking at us from all sides!
In the sky, along the shore,
out to sea...the sky is smiling!
Oh, lovely night!
In a ecstasy of love
the sky is smiling!

Act 2

INSIDE BUTTERFLY'S HOUSE

disc no. 1/track 14 Act II begins with an impatient motive in the solo flute, taken over first by high strings, then low strings. Two clarinets then lead us up to a tragic motive **(00:43)** before Suzuki, tired of the trials they have endured for three years, dutifully says her prayers to a plodding string accompaniment. A second tragic motive is heard at the close of her prayer **(01:56)**

(Suzuki is praying in front of a statue of Buddha, occasionally ringing the prayer-bell. Butterfly is standing, erect and immobile, by a screen.)

SUZUKI
E Izaghi e Izanami,
sarundasico e Kami...
Oh! la mia testa!
E tu, Ten-Sjoo-daj!
Fate che Butterfly
non pianga più, mai più.

BUTTERFLY
Pigri ed obesi
son gli dei giapponesi!
L'americano Iddio,
son persuasa,
ben più presto risponde
a chi l'implori.
Ma temo ch'egli ignori
che noi stiam qui di casa.

SUZUKI
Izaghi, Izanami,
sarundasico Kami...
Oh, my head!
And thou, Ten-Sjoo-daj,
don't let Butterfly
cry any more, any more.

BUTTERFLY
Fat and lazy
are the gods of Japan.
The American God,
I'm sure,
is much quicker in answering
those who pray to him.
But I'm afraid he may not know
we have our home here.

Suzuki...
è lungi la miseria?

Suzuki... how long will it be before we run
out of money?

(Suzuki opens a little table, takes out a few coins and shows them to Butterfly.)

SUZUKI
Questo è l'ultimo fondo.

SUZUKI
This is all we have left.

BUTTERFLY
Questo? Oh! troppe spese!

BUTTERFLY
This? Oh! We've been too extravagant!

SUZUKI
S'egli non torna e presto,
siamo male in arnese.

SUZUKI
If he doesn't come back, and soon,
we shall be in a bad way.

BUTTERFLY
Ma torna.

BUTTERFLY
But he will come back!

SUZUKI
Tornerà?

SUZUKI
He will come back?

BUTTERFLY
Perché dispone che il Console
provveda alla pigione,
rispondi, su!
Perché con tante cure
la casa rifornì di serrature,
s'ei non volesse ritornar mai più?

BUTTERFLY
Why does he arrange for the Consul
to look after the rent?
Tell me, quick!
Why did he take such care to have
the house fitted with locks
if he didn't mean to come back again?

SUZUKI
Non lo so.

SUZUKI
I don't know.

BUTTERFLY
Non lo sai?
Io te lo dico
per tener ben fuori le zanzare,
i parenti ed i dolori,

BUTTERFLY
You don't know?
I'll tell you then:
in order to keep mosquitos,
relations and troubles outside,

e dentro, con gelosa custodia,
la sua sposa -
la sua sposa che son io, Butterfly!

SUZUKI
Ma non s'è udito
di straniero marito
che sia tornato al suo nido.

BUTTERFLY
Ah! taci, o t'uccido.
Quell'ultima mattina:
"Tornerete signor?"
gli domandai.
Egli, col cuore grosso,
per celarmi la pena
sorridendo rispose:
"O Butterfly,
piccina mogliettina,
tornerò colle rose
alla stagion serena
quando fa la nidiata
il pettirosso."
Tornerà.

SUZUKI
Speriam.

BUTTERFLY
Dillo con me:
tornerà.

SUZUKI
Tornerà.

and inside, jealously guarded,
his bride -
his bride - me - Butterfly!

SUZUKI
No one has ever heard
of a foreign husband
returning to his home.

BUTTERFLY
Be quiet, or I'll kill you!
On that last morning,
"Are you coming back, sir?"
I asked him.
With a heavy heart,
trying to hide his unhappiness from me,
smiling he replied:
"Oh, Butterfly,
my dear sweet little wife,
I'll return with the roses
in that happy season
when the robin
builds his nest."
He'll come back.

SUZUKI
Let us hope so.

BUTTERFLY
Say it with me.
He'll come back.

SUZUKI
He'll come back.

BUTTERFLY

Piangi? Perché? Perché?
Ah, la fede ti manca!
Senti;
Un bel dì vedremo
levarsi un fil di fumo
sull'estremo confin del mare.
E poi la nave appare -
poi la nave bianca
entra nel porto, romba
il suo saluto. Vedi?
È venuto!
Io non gli scendo incontro.
Io no. Mi metto là
sul ciglio del colle e aspetto,
e aspetto gran tempo
e non mi pesa
la lunga attesa.
E uscito dalla folla cittadina
un uom, un picciol punto
s'avvia per la collina.
Chi sarà? chi sarà?
E come sarà giunto -
Che dirà? che dirà?
Chiamerà "Butterfly!"
dalla lontana.
Io senza dar risposta
me ne starò nascosta,
un po' per celia
e un po' per non morir
al primo incontro,
ed egli alquanto in pena
chiamerà, chiamerà:

BUTTERFLY

You're crying? Whatever for?
Oh, you are lacking in faith!
Listen.
One fine day we'll see
a wisp of smoke arising
over the extreme verge of the sea's horizon,
and afterwards the ship will appear.
Then the white ship
will enter the harbour, will thunder
a salute. You see?
He's arrived!
I shan't go down to meet him.
No, I shall stand there
on the brow of the hill and wait,
and wait a long time,
and I shan't find
the long wait wearisome.
And from the midst of the city crowd
a man - a tiny speck -
will make his way up the hill.
Who can it be?
And when he arrives -
what, what will he say?
He'll call, "Butterfly!"
from the distance.
Not answering, I'll
remain hidden,
partly to tease,
and partly so as not to die
at the first meeting.
And, a trifle worried,
he'll call, he'll call

"Piccina mogliettina,
olezzo di verbena!" -
i nomi che mi dava
al suo venire.
Tutto questo avverrà,
te lo prometto.
Tienti la tua paura,
io con sicura fede l'aspetto.

"My dear little wife,
fragrance of verbena!" -
the names he used to call me
when he came here.
And this will happen,
I promise you.
Keep your fears;
with unalterable faith I shall wait for him.

(She dismisses Suzuki, who leaves. Sharpless and Goro can be seen entering the garden.)

GORO
C'è. Entrate.

GORO
She's there. Go in.

SHARPLESS
Chiedo scusa...Madama Butterfly...

SHARPLESS
Excuse me...Madam Butterfly...

BUTTERFLY
Madama Pinkerton, prego.

BUTTERFLY
Madam Pinkerton, please.

(She turns round.)

Oh! il mio signor Console,
signor Console!

Oh! My dear consul,
my dear sir!

SHARPLESS
Mi ravvisate?

SHARPLESS
You remember me?

BUTTERFLY
Ben venuto in casa americana.

BUTTERFLY
Welcome to an American house.

SHARPLESS
Grazie.

SHARPLESS
Thank you.

BUTTERFLY
Avi, antenati - tutti bene?

SHARPLESS
Ma, spero.

BUTTEFLY
Fumate?

(She beckons to Suzuki to prepare the pipe.)

SHARPLESS
Grazie. Ho qui...

BUTTERFLY
Signore, io vedo il cielo azzurro.

HARPLESS
Grazie. Ho...

BUTTERFLY
Preferite forse le sigarette
 americane?

SHARPLESS
Grazie. Ho da mostrarvi...

BUTTERFLY *(porgendo un fiammifero acceso)*
A voi.

SHARPLESS
Mi scrisse Benjamin Franklin Pinkerton.

BUTTERFLY
Davvero! È in salute?

BUTTERFLY
Your grandparents and ancestors are quite
well?

SHARPLESS
I sincerely hope so.

BUTTERFLY
Will you smoke?

SHARPLESS
Thank you. I have here...

BUTTERFLY
Sir, I see the skies are blue.

SHARPLESS
No thank you. I have...

BUTTERFLY
Perhaps you would prefer American cigarettes?

SHARPLESS
Thank you. I have to show you...

BUTTERFLY *(offering Sharpless a light)*
Here you are.

SHARPLESS
Benjamin Franklin Pinkerton has written
to me...

BUTTERFLY
Really! Is he quite well?

SHARPLESS
Perfetta.

BUTTERFLY
Io son la donna più lieta del Giappone.
Potrei farvi una domanda?

SHARPLESS
Certo.

BUTTERFLY
Quando fanno il lor nido
in America i pettirossi?

SHARPLESS
Come dite?

BUTTERFLY
Sì...prima o dopo di qui?

SHARPLESS
Ma...perché?

BUTTERFLY
Mio marito m'ha promesso
di ritornar nella stagion beata
che il pettirosso rifà la nidiata.
Qui l'ha rifatta
per ben tre volte, ma può darsi
che di là usi nidiar men spesso.
Chi ride?
Oh, c'è il nakodo.
Un uom cattivo.

GORO
Godo...

SHARPLESS
Perfectly.

BUTTERFLY
I am the happiest woman in Japan.
May I ask you a question?

SHARPLESS
Certainly.

BUTTERFLY
When do the robins make their nests
in America?

SHARPLESS
What did you say?

BUTTERFLY
Yes...before or after they do here?

SHARPLESS
But...why?

BUTTERFLY
My husband promised
to return in that happy season
when the robin builds his nest again.
Here, it has done so
three times already, but it may be
that over there it doesn't nest so often.
Who's that laughing?
Oh, it's the marriage-broker.
A bad man.

GORO
I am enjoying...

BUTTERFLY
Zitto.

(to Sharpless)

Egli osò...
No, prima rispondete alla domanda mia.

SHARPLESS
Mi rincresce, ma ignoro...
non ho studiato ornitologia.

BUTTERFLY
Orni...

SHARPLESS
tologia.

BUTTERFLY
Non lo sapete insomma.

BUTTERFLY
Be quiet.

He dared...
No, first answer my question.

SHARPLESS
I'm sorry, but I don't know.
I haven't studied ornithology.

BUTTERFLY
Orni...

SHARPLESS
...thology.

BUTTERFLY
So you don't know, then.

disc no. 1/track 17 Now we first hear the music associated with Butterfly's suitor, Yamadori **(00:48)**. This jolly oriental tune is contrasted with the soaring phrases of Butterfly's mocking response to his royal offer of marriage **(01:02)**.

SHARPLESS
No. Dicevamo...

BUTTERFLY
Ah sì, Goro, appena
B. F. Pinkerton fu in mare,
mi venne ad assediare
con ciarle e con presenti
per ridarmi ora questo,
or quel marito.
Or promette tesori
per uno scimunito...

SHARPLESS
No. We were saying...

BUTTERFLY
Ah, yes... Goro, as soon as
B. F. Pinkerton was at sea,
he came annoying me
with gossip and presents,
offering me first this one,
then that one in second marriage.
Now he's promising me riches
from a silly idiot.

GORO
Il ricco Yamadori.
Ella è povera in canna.
I suoi parenti
l'han tutti rinnegata.

GORO
The rich Yamadori.
She hasn't a penny.
Her relations
have all renounced her.

(Beyond the terrace Yamadori can be seen approaching on a palanquin, surrounded by servants.)

BUTTERFLY
Eccolo. Attenti.
Yamadori...
Ancor le pene dell'amor
non v'han deluso?
Vi tagliate ancor le vene
se il mio bacio vi ricuso?

BUTTERFLY
There he is. Look.
Yamadori...
aren't you disillusioned
with love's pains yet?
Do you still intend to cut your veins
if I refuse you a kiss?

YAMADORI
Tra le cose più moleste
è inutil sospirar.

YAMADORI
One of the most annoying things
is hopeless sighing.

BUTTERFLY
Tante mogli omai toglieste,
vi doveste abituar.

BUTTERFLY
You've had so many wives by now
you must be used to it.

YAMADORI
L'ho sposate tutte quante
e il divorzio mi francò.

YAMADORI
I married them, one and all,
and divorce has set me free.

BUTTERFLY
Obbligata.

BUTTERFLY
Most obliged.

disc. no. 2/track 1 Butterfly declares her independence from Japanese law to the strains of "The Star Spangled Banner" **(00:46)**, and after refusing Yamadori's advances, she serves tea to the accompaniment of a decidedly Western-sounding waltz **(02:00)**

YAMADORI
A voi però giurerei
fede costante.

SHARPLESS
Il messaggio, ho gran paura,
a trasmetter non riesco.

GORO
Ville, servi, oro, ad Omara
un palazzo principesco.

BUTTERFLY
Già legata è la mia fede.

GORO E YAMADORI (a Sharpless)
Maritata ancor si crede.

BUTTERFLY
Non mi credo. Sono, sono.

GORO
Ma la legge...

BUTTERFLY
Io non la so.

GORO
Per la moglie, l'abbandono
al divorzio equiparò...

BUTTERFLY
La legge giapponese...
non già del mio paese.

GORO
Quale?

YAMADORI
But to you I would vow
to be faithful.

SHARPLESS
I'm afraid I shan't succeed
in delivering the message...

GORO
Villas, servants, gold, and at Omara
a princely palace!

BUTTERFLY
My troth is plighted already.

GORO AND YAMADORI (TO SHARPLESS)
She thinks she's married.

BUTTERFLY
I don't think so - I am. I am.

GORO
But the law...

BUTTERFLY
I don't know anything about that.

GORO
...for the wife has made desertion
equivalent to divorce.

BUTTERFLY
The Japanese law...
not that of my country now.

GORO
Which country?

BUTTERFLY
Gli Stati Uniti.

SHARPLESS
Oh, l'infelice!

BUTTERFLY
Si sa che aprir la porta
e la moglie cacciar
per la più corta
qui divorziar si dice.
Ma in America questo non si può -

(to Sharpless)

Vero?

SHARPLESS
Vero...Però...

BUTTERFLY
Là un bravo giudice serio,
impettito dice al marito:
"Lei vuol andarsene?
Sentiam perché?"
"Sono seccato
del coniugato."
E il magistrato:
"Ah, mascalzone,
presto in prigione."
Suzuki, il thè.

YAMADORI
Udiste?

BUTTERFLY
The United States.

SHARPLESS
Poor thing!

BUTTERFLY
We're quite aware that to open the door
and chase out the wife
with no further ado
is called divorce here.
But in America you can't do that.

Can you?

SHARPLESS
No. But...

BUTTERFLY
There, a good judge, grave
and upright, says to the husband:
"You want to go away?
Let us hear why?"
"I'm bored
with married life!"
And the magistrate:
"You rascal,
into prison with you, quick!"
Tea, Suzuki.

YAMADORI
You heard?

SHARPLESS
Mi rattrista
una sì piena cecità.

GORO
Segnalata è già
la nave di Pinkerton.

YAMADORI
Quand'essa lo riveda...

SHARPLESS
Egli non vuol mostrarsi.
Io venni appunto
per levarla d'inganno...

BUTTERFLY
Vostra Grazia permette...
che persone moleste!

YAMADORI
Addio. Vi lascio
il cuor pien di cordoglio:
ma spero ancor...

BUTTERFLY
Padrone.

YAMADORI
Ah, se voleste...

BUTTERFLY
Il guaio è che non voglio...

SHARPLESS
Such utter
blindness grieves me deeply.

GORO
Pinkerton's ship
is already signalled.

YAMADORI
When she sees him again...

SHARPLESS
He doesn't wish to show himself.
I have come expressly
to relieve her of any illusions on that score.

BUTTERFLY
If your Grace will allow...
What tiresome people!

YAMADORI
Farewell. I leave you
with my heart full of grief,
but I still hope...

BUTTERFLY
Please yourself.

YAMADORI
Oh, if only you would...

BUTTERFLY
The trouble is, I don't want to.

(Yamadori leaves. Goro follows him.)

disc. no. 2/track 2 Finally, Sharpless gets the chance to read Pinkerton's letter to Butterfly, and the moment is accompanied by our first hearing of the music of the Humming Chorus **(01:01)**, which will accompany her patient vigil at the close of the scene. Struck by Sharpless's suggestion that Pinkerton may not return, Butterfly sings in short, separated phrases, exploring her options **(03:34)**. Concluding that she would prefer death, the truncated phrases become a funeral march.

SHARPLESS
Ora a noi.
Sedete qui.
Legger con me
volete questa lettera?

BUTTERFLY
Date.

SHARPLESS
Our turn now.
Sit down here.
Will you read
this letter with me?

BUTTERFLY
Give it to me.

(She takes it and kisses it, then gives it back to the Consul.)

Sulla bocca, sul cuore...
Siete l'uomo migliore del mondo.
Incominciate.

To my lips, on my heart...
You're the kindest man in the whole world.
Please begin.

SHARPLESS
"Amico, cercherete
quel bel fiore di fanciulla..."

SHARPLESS
"My dear friend, will you go and see
that pretty flower of a girl..."

BUTTERFLY
Dice proprio così?

BUTTERFLY
Does he really say that?

SHARPLESS
Sì, così dice,
ma se ad ogni momento...

SHARPLESS
Yes, he does,
but if every moment...

BUTTERFLY
Taccio, taccio,
più nulla...

BUTTERFLY
I'll keep quiet, I'll keep quiet.
I won't interrupt any more.

SHARPLESS
"Da quel tempo felice
tre anni son passati..."

BUTTERFLY
Anche lui li ha contati!

SHARPLESS
"E forse Butterfly
non mi rammenta più."

BUTTERFLY
Non lo rammento?
Suzuki, dillo tu.
"Non mi rammenta più."

SHARPLESS
Pazienza!
"Se mi vuol bene ancor,
se m'aspetta..."

BUTTERFLY
Oh, le dolci parole!
Tu, benedetta!

SHARPLESS
"A voi mi raccomando perché vogliate
con circospezione prepararla..."

BUTTERFLY
Ritorna...

SHARPLESS
"...Al colpo."

BUTTERFLY
Quando? Presto! Presto!

SHARPLESS
"Since that happy time
three years have gone by..."

BUTTERFLY
He's counted them, too!

SHARPLESS
"And perhaps Butterfly
does not remember me any more."

BUTTERFLY
Not remember him?
 - Suzuki, tell him.
"Does not remember me any more..."

SHARPLESS
Patience!
"If she still loves me,
if she expects me..."

BUTTERFLY
Oh, what sweet words!
You blessed, blessed letter!

SHARPLESS
"I beg you to be so good as,
with tact, to prepare her gently..."

BUTTERFLY
He's coming.

SHARPLESS
"... for the blow."

BUTTERFLY
When? Quick! Quick!

SHARPLESS (*fre sé*)
Benone.
Qui troncarla conviene.
Quel diavolo d'un Pinkerton!

(*to Butterfly*)

Ebbene, che fareste,
Madama Butterfly,
s'ei non dovesse ritornar
più mai?

BUTTERFLY
Due cose potrei far:
tornar a divertir la gente
col cantar...oppur...
meglio, morire.

SHARPLESS
Di strapparvi assai mi costa
dai miraggi ingannatori.
Accogliete la proposta
di quel ricco Yamadori.

BUTTERFLY
Voi, signor, mi dite questo! Voi!

SHARPLESS
Santo Dio, come si fa?

BUTTERFLY
Qui, Suzuki, presto, presto,
che Sua Grazia se ne va.

SHARPLESS
Mi scacciate?

SHARPLESS (*to himself*)
This is fine, I must say!
I must break it to her without more ado.
That devil of a Pinkerton!

Well now, what would you do,
Madam Butterfly,
if he were never
to return?

BUTTERFLY
I could do one of two things:
go back to entertaining people
with my songs;
or better, die.

SHARPLESS
It grieves me deeply to rob you
of your illusions.
Accept the proposal
of the wealthy Yamadori.

BUTTERFLY
You! You, sir, tell me this! You!

SHARPLESS
Great God, what am I to do?

BUTTERFLY
Come here quickly, Suzuki.
His Grace is going.

SHARPLESS
Are you turning me out?

BUTTERFLY
Ve ne prego,
già l'insistere non vale.

SHARPLESS
Fui brutale,
non lo nego.

BUTTERFLY
Oh, mi fate tanto male,
tanto male, tanto, tanto!
Niente, niente! Ho creduto morir...
Ma passa presto come passan
le nuvole sul mare...
Ah! m'ha scordata?

BUTTERFLY
Please,
forget what I said.

SHARPLESS
I was brutal,
I don't deny it.

BUTTERFLY
Oh, you hurt me so much,
so much, so very much!
It's nothing, nothing! I thought I was going
to die,
but it soon passes like
clouds over the sea...
Has he forgotten me, then?

(Going into the inner room, she returns with a child in her arms.)

disc no. 2/track 3 As Butterfly runs from the room to fetch her son, she is accompanied by a theme which brings together a motive from "The Star Spangled Banner" and the act I love duet. Upon her return, we hear a Japanese-sounding theme which will continue to be associated with the child **(00:17)**

E questo? E questo?
E questo egli potrà pure scordare?

SHARPLESS
Egli è suo?

BUTTERFLY
Chi vide mai a bimbo
di Giappon occhi azzurrini?
E il labbro?
E i ricciolini d'oro schietto?

And this? And this?
Can he forget this as well?

SHARPLESS
It is his?

BUTTERFLY
Whoever saw a
Japanese child with blue eyes?
And his mouth?
And his curls of pure gold?

SHARPLESS
È palese. E Pinkerton lo sa?

SHARPLESS
It's obvious. And does Pinkerton know?

disc no. 2/track 4 *Che tua madre.* Butterfly addresses this aria to her child, and we hear the "geisha" theme **(00:37)** as she describes what their lives would be like if she returned to her former livelihood.

BUTTERFLY
No. No. È nato
quand'egli stava in quel
suo gran paese. Ma voi...
gli scriverete.
Che l'aspetta un figlio
senza pari!
E mi saprete dir
s'ei non s'affretta
per le terre e pei mari!
Sai cos'ebbe cuore
di pensar quel signore?
Che tua madre dovrà
prenderti in braccio
ed alla pioggia e al vento
andar per la città
a guadagnarti
il pane e il vestimento.
Ed alle impietosite genti
la man tremante stenderà
gridando, "Udite, udite
la triste mia canzon.
A un'infelice madre
la carità, muovetevi a pietà."
E Butterfly, orribile destino,
danzerà per te!
E come fece già
la ghescia canterà.
E la canzon giuliva e lieta
in un singhiozzo finirà.

BUTTERFLY
No, no. The child was born
after he'd gone back
to that great country of his. But you
will write him
that a son without equal
is waiting for him here!
And then you'll see
if he doesn't come hurrying
over the land and sea!
Do you know what that gentleman
had the heart to think?
That your mother would have
to take you in her arms
and in all weathers
walk the city streets
to earn you
food and clothing,
and to the pitying crowd
stretch out a trembling hand,
crying, "Listen, listen
to my sad tale.
Charity for an unhappy mother!
Have pity!"
And Butterfly - oh, horrible fate -
will dance for you!
And as she used to do,
the geisha will sing!
And the gay and merry song
will end in a sob!

Ah, no! no! questo mai!
Questo mestier
che al disonore porta!
Morta! morta! Mai più danzar!
Piuttosto la mia vita vo' troncar!
Ah! morta!

SHARPLESS *(fra sé)*
Quanta pietà.

(to Butterfly)

Io scendo al piano.
Mi perdonate?

BUTTERFLY
A te, dagli la mano.

SHARPLESS
I bei capelli biondi!
Caro, come ti chiamano?

BUTTERFLY
Rispondi:
Oggi il mio nome è Dolore.
Però, dite al babbo,
scrivendogli,
che il giorno del suo ritorno
Gioia, Gioia mi chiamerò.

SHARPLESS
Tuo padre lo saprà, te lo prometto.

(He leaves hurriedly.)

SUZUKI *(gridando da fuori)*
Vespa! Rospo maledetto!

Oh no, no, never!
Not that profession
which leads to dishonour!
Rather let me die! To dance no more!
I will cut my life short rather!
Oh, let me die!

SHARPLESS *(to himself)*
How pitiful!

I must go back now.
Will you forgive me?

BUTTERFLY
You... give him your hand.

SHARPLESS
What pretty fair curls!
What is your name, darling?

BUTTERFLY
Answer:
My name is Sorrow now.
But when you write
to Daddy tell him
that the day he comes back
I shall be called Joy, Joy!

SHARPLESS
Your father shall know it. I promise you.

SUZUKI *(shouting outside)*
Serpent! Accursed toad!

(She comes in, dragging Goro by the ear.)

BUTTERFLY
Che fu?

SUZUKI
Ci ronza intorno
il vampiro! e ogni giorno
ai quattro venti spargendo va
che niuno sa chi padre
al bimbo sia!

GORO
Dicevo...solo...
che là in America
quando un figliuolo è nato maledetto
trarrà sempre reietto
la vita fra le genti!

BUTTERFLY
Ah! tu menti! menti!
Dillo ancora e t'uccido!

SUZUKI
No!

BUTTERFLY
Va via!
Vedrai, piccolo amor,
mia pena e mio conforto,
mio piccolo amor,
Ah! vedrai che il tuo vendicator
ci porterà lontano, lontan,
nella sua terra...lontan ci porterà.

BUTTERFLY
What's happened?

SUZUKI
He buzzes round us,
the vampire! And every day
to the four winds he spreads abroad
that nobody knows
who the baby's father is!

GORO
I only said
that over there in America
when a child is born so unfortunate
he will always be an outcast
among people!

BUTTERFLY
Ah! you lie! you lie! you lie!
Say it again and I'll kill you!

SUZUKI
No!

BUTTERFLY
Get out!
You'll see, my little love,
my sorrow and my comfort,
my little love,
oh, you will see, your avenger will
take us far, far away
to his own country...he'll take us far away.

(A cannon is heard.)

disc no. 2/track 7 As we hear the aria Un bel di again in the orchestra, Butterfly scans the horizon for Pinkerton's ship. She is vindicated. Her dream is coming true.

SUZUKI
Il cannone del porto!
Una nave da guerra...

SUZUKI
The harbour gun!
A warship!

BUTTERFLY
Bianca...bianca...il vessillo
americano delle stelle...
Or governa per ancorare.

BUTTERFLY
It's white... white... the American flag!
with the stars...
Now it's manoeuvring to drop anchor.

(She takes the telescope.)

disc no. 2/track 8 Butterfly and Suzuki decorate the house for Pinkerton's arrival. Puccini was accused of using a Viennese operetta style in this piece. Even if he did, the lesser style in the hands of such a master created one of opera's most endearing moments.

Reggimi la mano
ch'io discerna il nome,
il nome, il nome...
Eccolo: Abramo Lincoln!
Tutti han mentito!
Sol io lo sapevo,
sol io che l'amo.
Vedi lo scimunito tuo dubbio?
È giunto! è giunto!
Proprio nel punto
che ognun diceva:
piangi e dispera.
Trionfa il mio amor! il mio amor!
La mia fè trionfa intera.
Ei torna e m'ama!
Scuoti quella fronda di ciliegio
e m'innonda di fior.

Steady my hand
so that I can see the name...
the name, the name...
There it is: Abraham Lincoln!
They all lied! The lot of them!
I alone knew...
Only I who love him.
Do you see how foolish your doubts were?
He's come! He's come! He's come!
Just at the very moment
when everybody said:
weep and despair!
My love triumphs, yes, triumphs!
My faith is completely vindicated!
He has come back and he loves me!
Shake that branch of the cherry tree
and rain down

blooms on me.

Io vò tuffar
nella pioggia odorosa
l'arsa fronte.

SUZUKI
Signora, quietatevi...quel pianto.

BUTTERFLY
No, rido, rido!
Quanto lo dovremo aspettar?
Che pensi? Un'ora?

SUZUKI
Di più.

BUTTTERLY
Due ore forse.
Tutto...tutto...
sia pien di fior, come
la notte è di faville.
Va pei fior.

SUZUKI
Tutti i fior?

BUTTERFLY
Tutti i fior, tutti, tutti.
Pesco, viola, gelsomin,
quanto di cespo, o d'erba,
o d'albero fiorì.

SUZUKI
Uno squallor d'inverno
sarà tutto il giardin.

I want to plunge
my burning brow in its fragrant rain.

SUZUKI
Madam, calm yourself...those tears...

BUTTERFLY
No, no, I'm laughing!
How long shall we have to wait for him?
What do you think? An hour?

SUZUKI
Longer.

BUTTERFLY
Two hours, maybe.
Everywhere
must be full of flowers,
as the night is of stars.
Go and pick the flowers!

SUZUKI
All of them?

BUTTERFLY
All of them, all, all.
Peach blossom, violets, jasmine -
every bush, plant
and tree that's in flower!

SUZUKI
The whole garden will be
as desolate as winter.

BUTTERFLY
Tutta la primavera
voglio che olezzi qui.

SUZUKI
Uno squallor d'inverno
sarà tutto il giardin.
A voi, signora.

BUTTERFLY
Cogline ancora.

SUZUKI
Sovente a questa siepe
veniste a riguardare lungi,
piangendo nella deserta immensità.

BUTTERFLY
Giunse l'atteso,
nulla più chiedo al mare;
diedi pianto alla zolla,
essa i suoi fior mi dà.

SUZUKI
Spoglio è l'orto.

BUTTERFLY
Spoglio è l'orto?
Vien, m'aiuta.

SUZUKI
Rose al varco della soglia.

BUTTERFLY
Tutta la primavera
voglio che olezzi qui.

BUTTERFLY
I want all the perfume
of spring in here.

SUZUKI
The whole garden will be
as desolate as winter.
Here you are, Madam.

BUTTERFLY
Pick some more.

SUZUKI
You used to come to this hedge
so often to gaze in tears,
far out over the empty expanse.

BUTTERFLY
The long-awaited one has come,
I ask nothing more of the sea,
I gave tears to the soil,
it gives its flowers to me!

SUZUKI
The garden's bare.

BUTTERFLY
Is it? Then come
and help me.

SUZUKI
Roses at the entrance to the threshold.

BUTTERFLY
I want all the perfume of spring
in here.

BUTTERFLY E **SUZUKI**
Seminiamo intorno april.

SUZUKI
Gigli? viole?

BUTTERFLY
Intorno spandi...
Il suo sedil s'inghirlandi
di convolvi, gigli e rose.

BUTTERFLY E **SUZUKI**
Gettiamo a mani piene
mammole e tuberose,
corolle di verbene,
petali d'ogni fior!

BUTTERFLY
Or vienmi ad adornar.
No, pria portami il bimbo.
Non son più quella!
Troppi sospiri la bocca mandò...
E l'occhio riguardò
nel lontan troppo fiso.
Dammi sul viso
un tocco di carminio...
Ed anche a te, piccino,
perché la veglia
non ti faccia vôte
per pallore le gote.

SUZUKI
Non vi movete
che v'ho a ravviare i capelli.

BUTTERFLY
Che ne diranno!

BUTTERFLY AND **SUZUKI**
Let us sow April all about us.

SUZUKI
Lilies? Violets?

BUTTERFLY
Scatter lilies and violets all about us!
His chair let us twine
with flower garlands!

BUTTERFLY AND **SUZUKI**
By the handful let's scatter
violets and tuberoses,
blossoms of verbena,
petals of every flower!

BUTTERFLY
Now, come and dress me.
But no! First bring me the baby.
I'm no longer what I was.
These lips have breathed too many sighs...
and these eyes have gazed
too hard into the distance.
Give my face
a touch of rouge...
and you too, little one,
so that the long wait
won't leave your cheeks
pale and hollow.

SUZUKI
Keep still,
I have to do your hair.

BUTTERFLY
What will they say now?

E lo zio Bonzo?	And my uncle, the Bonze?
Già del mio danno	All of them so glad
tutti contenti!	at my sad plight!
E Yamadori coi suoi languori!	And Yamadori, with his languishing!
Beffati, scornati,	Ridiculed, disgraced,
spennati gli ingrati!	shown up, the unkind creatures!

SUZUKI
È fatto.

SUZUKI
I've finished.

BUTTERFLY
L'obi che vestii da sposa.
Qua, ch'io lo vesta.
Vo' che mi veda indosso
il vel del primo dì.
E un papavero rosso
nei capelli...Così.
nello shosi or farem tre forellini
per riguardar,
e starem zitti come topolini
ad aspettar.

BUTTERFLY
The sash I wore as a bride.
Bring it here for me to put on.
I want him to see me dressed
as I was that first day.
And a red poppy
in my hair... like that.
Now we'll make three little holes
in the paper screen to look through,
and we'll stay quiet as mice,
waiting.

(Butterfly leads the baby to the soshi and makes three holes in it; Suzuki sits on her haunches and looks out. Butterfly places herself in front of the biggest hole, and looking outside remains motionless and rigid as a statue. The baby is between his mother and Suzuki, and looks outside curiously. Night has fallen. Moon beams light up the soshi from outside. From far away voices can be heard humming.)

disc no. 2/track 10 The Humming Chorus is one of the most prized of the operatic choruses. The plaintive, wordless melody is heartrending in its simplicity.

Coro a bocca chiusa

Humming chorus

It is dawn. Butterfly still stands watching, motionless. The baby and Susuki are asleep. Sailor's voices are heard from the harbour below.

disc no. 2/track 11 The second scene of act II begins with an extended orchestral Intermezzo in which we seem to follow Butterfly's thoughts during her long vigil. It begins with a fortissimo statement of one of the themes associated with ill-fortune. This is followed by the melody from the act I when Butterfly kisses Pinkerton's hand **(00:56)**. It gives way to a new, beautiful and aching melody which seems to reflect Butterfly's longing for her husband's return **(01:28)**. This melody grows and modulates, culminating in a triumphant quote from the act I love duet and a whole series of quoted themes from earlier in the opera. As the music calms, we hear the sailors calling to one another in the harbor **(04:44)**, and finally the orchestration reflects the sun rising over the water **(05:46)**

VOCI DEI MARINAI *(da lontano)*
Oh eh! Oh eh! Oh eh!

SAILORS VOICES *(from afar)*
Oh eh! Oh eh! Oh eh!

disc no. 2/track 12 The triumphant theme we heard when the child, Sorrow, was first introduced now becomes a lullaby as Butterfly puts him to bed **(00:23)**

SUZUKI
Già il sole!
Cio-Cio-San...

SUZUKI
The sun's up already!
Cho-Cho-San!

BUTTERFLY
Verrà...verrà col pieno sole.

BUTTERFLY
He'll come... he'll come, you'll see.

SUZUKI
Salite a riposare, affranta siete.
Al suo venire vi chiamerò.

SUZUKI
Go and rest, you're tired out...
When he arrives I'll call you.

BUTTERFLY
Dormi, amor mio,
dormi sul mio cor.
Tu sei con Dio,
ed io col mio dolor.
A te i rai

BUTTERFLY
Sleep, my love,
sleep on my heart.
You are with God,
 and I'm with my sorrow.
On you shine the rays

degli astri d'or,
bimbo mio, dormi.

SUZUKI
Povera Butterfly!

BUTTERFLY
Dormi, amor mio,
dormi sul mio cor.
Tu sei con Dio,
ed io col mio dolor.

SUZUKI
Povera Butterfly!
Chi sia?
Oh!

of the golden stars...
Sleep, my child.

SUZUKI
Poor Butterfly!

BUTTERFLY
Sleep, my love,
sleep on my heart.
You are with god,
and I'm with my sorrow.

SUZUKI
Poor Butterfly!
Who can that be?
Oh!

(Pinkerton and Sharpless enter.)

PINKERTON
Zitta! Zitta! Non la destare.

SUZUKI
Era stanca, sì tanto!
Vi stette ad aspettare
tutta la notte col bimbo.

PINKERTON
Come sapea...?

SUZUKI
Non giunge da tre anni
una nave nel porto
che da lunge Butterfly
non ne scruti il color, la bandiera.

PINKERTON
Hush! Hush! Don't wake her.

SUZUKI
She was quite worn out!
She has been standing waiting for you
all night long with the baby.

PINKERTON
How did she know?

SUZUKI
For three years now
no ship has put into the harbour
without Butterfly scrutinising
its colour and flag from afar.

SHARPLESS (*a Pinkerton*)
Ve lo dissi?

SUZUKI
La chiamo...

PINKERTON
No, non ancor.

SUZUKI
Lo vedete, ier sera,
la stanza volle sparger
di fiori.

SHARPLESS
Ve lo dissi?

PINKERTON
Che pena!

SUZUKI
Chi c'è là fuori nel giardino?

PINKERTON
Zitta!

SUZUKI
Chi è? Chi è?

SHARPLESS
Meglio dirle ogni cosa.

SUZUKI
Chi è? Chi è?

SHARPLESS (*to Pinkerton*)
I told you, didn't I?

SUZUKI
I'll call her...

PINKERTON
No, not yet.

SUZUKI
You see, last night
she insisted on strewing
flowers all over the room.

SHARPLESS
I told you, didn't I?

PINKERTON
This is dreadful!

SUZUKI
Who's that out there in the garden?
It's a woman!

PINKERTON
Hush!

SUZUKI
Who is it? Who is it?

SHARPLESS
Best tell her everything.

SUZUKI
Who is it? Who is it?

PINKERTON
È venuta con me.

SUZUKI
Chi è? Chi è?

SHARPLESS
È sua moglie.

SUZUKI
Anime sante degli avi!
Alla piccina
s'è spento il sol!

SHARPLESS
Scegliemmo quest'ora mattutina
per ritrovarti sola, Suzuki,
e alla gran prova
un aiuto, un sostegno
cercar con te.

SUZUKI
Che giova? Che giova?

PINKERTON
She has come with me.

SUZUKI
Who is it? Who is it?

SHARPLESS
His wife.

SUZUKI
Holy spirits of my ancestors!
For the little one
the sun has gone out!

SHARPLESS
We chose this early hour
in order to find you alone, Suzuki,
and in this hour of trial
to seek some means of consolation
and support with you.

SUZUKI
What's the use? What's the use?

disc no. 2/track 14 *Io so che alle sue pene.* In this gorgeous trio, Puccini allows each of his characters to pour out their despair. The plodding motive in the low strings reflects the reluctant resignation of all three.

SHARPLESS
Io so che alle sue pene
non ci sono conforti.
Ma del bimbo conviene
assicurar le sorti.

SHARPLESS
I know that for her deep distress
there is no consolation.
But it is necessary to provide
for the child's future.

PINKERTON

Oh! l'amara fragranza
di questi fior
velenosa al cor mi va;
immutata è la stanza
dei nostri amor...

SHARPLESS

La pietosa
che entrar non osa
materna cura
del bimbo avrà.

SUZUKI

Oh, me trista!
E volete ch'io chieda
ad una madre...

SHARPLESS

Suvvia, parla con quella pia
e conducila qui...
S'anche la veda Butterfly,
non importa...anzi
meglio se accorta del vero
si facesse alla sua vista.
Vien, Suzuki, vien...

PINKERTON

Ma un gel di morte vi sta.
Il mio ritratto...
Tre anni son passati,
e noverati n'ha i giorni
e l'ore!
Non posso rimaner...
Sharpless, v'aspetto
per via...

PINKERTON

Oh, the bitter perfume
of these flowers
is poison to the heart!
The room where we loved
is unchanged...

SHARPLESS

That kind woman
who dares not enter
will care like a mother
for the child.

SUZUKI

Oh, I'm so miserable!
And you want me
to ask a mother...

SHARPLESS

Come, speak to that kind lady
and bring her in here.
Even if Butterfly should see her,
no matter... On the contrary,
better if she should realize
the truth through seeing her.
Come, Suzuki, come...

PINKERTON

But the coldness of death is in here.
My picture!...
Three years have passed,
and she has counted the days
and the hours!
I can't stay here...
Sharpless, I'll wait for you
on the way back...

SHARPLESS
Non ve l'avevo detto?

PINKERTON
Datele voi qualche soccorso...
Mi struggo dal rimorso.

SHARPLESS
Vel dissi? vi ricorda?
Badate, ella ci crede.
E fui profeta allor!
Sorda ai consigli,
sorda ai dubbi, vilipesa,
nell'ostinata attesa
raccolse il cor...

PINKERTON
Sì, tutto in un istante
io vede il fallo mio
e sento che di questo tormento
tregua mai non avrò.
No!

SHARPLESS
Andate.
Il triste vero
da sola apprenderà.

SHARPLESS
Didn't I tell you so?

PINKERTON
You give her some help...
I am completely crushed by remorse.

SHARPLESS
I told you! Do you remember?
When she gave you her hand,
"Beware!" I said, "she believes in all this!"
and my words were prophetic then!
Deaf to advice, deaf to all doubts, a victim
of scorn, obstinately waiting,
she fortified her heart.

PINKERTON
Yes, all in an instant
I see how I have sinned
and realise I shall never
find respite from this torture.
Never!

SHARPLESS
Go.
The sad truth
she'll learn alone.

disc no. 2/track 15 *Addio, fiorito asil.* This beautiful tenor aria was added to the score after the disastrous premiere, in order to balance the length of the final scene with the preceding scene, which are now separated by an intermission.

PINKERTON
Addio, fiorito asil
di letizia e d'amor...

PINKERTON
Farewell, flowery refuge
of happiness and love...

Sempre il mite suo sembiante
con strazio atroce vedrò.

SHARPLESS
Ma or quel cor sincero
presago è già...Vel dissi, ecc.

PINKERTON
Addio, fiorito asil...
Non reggo al tuo squallor...
Fuggo, fuggo...son vil!

SHARPLESS
Andate, il triste vero apprenderà.

Her sweet face will haunt me ever,
torturing me agonizingly.

SHARPLESS
But by now the faithful heart
maybe half suspects. I told you, etc.

PINKERTON
Farewell, flowery refuge...
I can't bear your desolation...
I must fly! I'm beneath contempt!

SHARPLESS
Go, she will learn the sad truth.

(Pinkerton hurries away as Kate and Suzuki come in from the garden.)

KATE
Glielo dirai?

SUZUKI
Prometto.

KATE
E le darai consiglio
d'affidarmi...

SUZUKI
Prometto.

KATE
Lo terrò come un figlio.

SUZUKI
Vi credo. Ma bisogna
ch'io le sia sola accanto...
nella grande ora...sola!

KATE
Will you tell her that?

SUZUKI
I promise.

KATE
And you'll advise her
to trust me?

SUZUKI
Yes.

KATE
I'll care for him like my own son.

SUZUKI
I believe you. But I must
be quite alone with her...
quite alone in this hour of crisis!

Piangerà tanto, tanto!	She'll cry so bitterly!

BUTTERFLY
Suzuki, Suzuki! Dove sei? Suzuki!
Suzuki, Suzuki! Dove sei?

BUTTERFLY
Suzuki! Suzuki! Where are you?
Suzuki!

SUZUKI
Son qui...
Pregavo e rimettevo
a posto...No...no...no...
Non scendete...no...no...

SUZUKI
Here I am...
I was praying tidying up...
No... no... no...
Don't come in... no... no...

disc no. 1/track 17 In halting phrases, Butterfly slowly realizes the truth and gradually becomes resigned to the surrender of her child. In long stately phrases she wishes her rival, Kate, all the happiness she deserves **(04:00)**, and when asked how the child will be turned over, Butterfly quotes from her own happy vision, *Un bel di,* saying Pinkerton should ascend the hill in half an hour to take the child **(05:08)**.

BUTTERFLY
È qui...è qui...
dove è nascosto?
È qui...è qui...
ecco il Console...
e...dove? dove?
Non c'è.
Quella donna!
Che vuol da me?
Niuno parla!
Perché piangete?
Non, non ditemi nulla...nulla...
Forse potrei cader morta sull'attimo...
Tu, Suzuki, che sei tanto buona,
non piangere!
E mi vuoi tanto bene -

BUTTERFLY
He's here, he's here...
where's he hidden?
He's here... he's here...
There's the Consul...
and where?... where?
He isn't here!
That woman?
What does she want at my house?
Nobody speaks!
Why are you crying?
No, don't tell me anything...
I might fall dead on the spot.
You, Suzuki, who are so good,
don't cry!
You love me so much -

un Sì, un No, di' piano:
vive?

SUZUKI
Sì.

BUTTERFLY
Ma non viene più.
Te l'han detto!
Vespa! voglio che tu risponda.

SUZUKI
Mai più.

BUTTERFLY
Ma è giunto ieri?

SUZUKI
Sì.

BUTTERFLY
Ah! quella donna
mi fa tanta paura!
tanta paura!

SHARPLESS
È la causa innocente
d'ogni vostra sciagura.
Perdonatele.

BUTTERFLY
Ah! è sua moglie!
Tutto è morto per me!
Tutto è finito!

yes or no - whisper...
Is he alive?

SUZUKI
Yes.

BUTTERFLY
But he won't come back any more.
They've told you?
Serpent! Will you answer me?

SUZUKI
Never again.

BUTTERFLY
But he arrived yesterday?

SUZUKI
Yes.

BUTTERFLY
Oh, that woman makes
me feel so afraid,
so afraid!

SHARPLESS
She is the innocent cause
of all your misfortunes.
Forgive her.

BUTTERFLY
Ah! she's his wife!
Everything is finished for me!
Everything is over! Oh!

SHARPLESS
Coraggio!

BUTTERFLY
Voglion prendermi tutto!
Il figlio mio!

SHARPLESS
Fatelo pel suo bene il sacrifizio.

BUTTERFLY
Ah! triste madre!
Abbandonar mio figlio!
E sia.
A lui devo obbedir!

KATE
Potete perdonarmi, Butterfly?

BUTTERFLY
Sotto il gran ponte del cielo
non v'è donna di voi più felice.
Siatelo sempre...
Non v'attristate per me...

KATE
Povera piccina!

SHARPLESS
È un'immensa pietà.

KATE
E il figlio lo darà?

BUTTERFLY
A lui lo potrò dare,
se lo verrà a cercare.

SHARPLESS
Be brave.

BUTTERFLY
They want to take everything
away from me! My son!

SHARPLESS
Make the sacrifice for his sake.

BUTTERFLY
Oh, unhappy mother!
To be obliged to give up my son!
Very well then!
I must obey him in everything.

KATE
Can you ever forgive me, Butterfly?

BUTTERFLY
Under the great dome of heaven,
there isn't a happier woman than you.
May you always be so...
Don't upset yourself about me...

KATE
Poor little thing!

SHARPLESS
It's a terrible shame!

KATE
And will she give up the child?

BUTTERFLY
I'll be able to give up the child to him,
if he'll come and fetch him.

Fra mezz'ora
salite la collina.

SUZUKI
Come una mosca prigioniera
l'ali batte il piccolo cuor!

BUTTERFLY
Troppa luce è di fuor,
e troppo primavera.
Chiudi.
Il bimbo ove sia?

SUZUKI
Giuoca...Lo chiamo?

BUTTERFLY
Lascialo giocar...
Va a fargli compagnia.

SUZUKI
Resto con voi.

BUTTERFLY
Va, va. Te lo comando.

Return up the hill
in half-an-hour's time.

SUZUKI
Like the wings of a captive fly
her little heart is beating!

BUTTERFLY
There's too much light outside,
and too much spring.
Close the screens to.
Where's the baby?

SUZUKI
He's playing...Shall I call him?

BUTTERFLY
Let him play...
Go and keep him company.

SUZUKI
I'll stay with you.

BUTTERFLY
Go along, I order you to.

(Suzuki goes out, crying. Butterfly lights a taper in front of the sanctuary, and bows. Then she takes her father's knife from the wall, kisses it, and slowly reads the inscription on the blade.)

disc no. 2/track 19 Again we hear the dagger theme as Butterfly takes it up and reads the inscription. Suddenly, Suzuki pushes the child into the room **(00:48)** and Butterfly sings her farewell, *Tu, Tu piccolo Iddio!* (You, Little Idol), accompanied by an upwardly surging motive **(01:52)** which dissolves in the end into a funeral march **(03:06)**. She stabs herself, and we hear Pinkerton's voice calling her in the distance. When he arrives on the scene, the full orchestra reiterates the "geisha" theme in B minor, ending the opera on a jarring G-major chord.

"Con onor muore
chi non può serbar vita con onore."

"He dies with honour
who cannot live with honour."

(As she places the blade against her throat, the door opens and Suzuki's arm pushes the child towards his mother. Butterfly drops the knife and rushes to the child, which she seizes up and kisses passionately.)

Tu? tu? tu? tu?
Piccolo iddio!
Amore, amore mio.
Fior di giglio e di rosa.
Non saperlo mai...per te,
pei tuoi puri occhi
muore Butterfly...
Perché tu possa andar
di là dal mare
senza che ti rimorda
ai dì maturi
il materno abbandono.
O a me, sceso dal trono
dell'alto Paradiso,
guarda ben fiso, fiso,
di tua madre la faccia!
Che ten' resti una traccia,
guarda ben!
Amore, addio, addio!
Piccolo amor!
Va, gioca, gioca.

You? You? You?
Little idol of my heart.
My Love, my love,
flower of the lily and rose.
Never know that, for you,
for your innocent eyes,
Butterfly is about to die...
so that you may go
away beyond the sea
without being subject to remorse
in later years
for your mother's desertion.
Oh, you who have come down to me
from high heaven,
look well, well
on your mother's face,
that you may keep a faint memory of it,
look well!
Little love, farewell!
Farewell, my little love!
Go and play.

(She picks up the child and sets him down on a mat; she gives him an American flag and a doll to play with and gently blindfolds his eyes. Picking up the knife she goes behind the screen. Then appearing from behind the screen with the white veil clasped round her throat, Butterfly staggers across the room towards the baby, and collapses beside him.)

VOCE DI PINKERTON
Butterfly! Butterfly! Butterfly!

VOICE OF PINKERTON
Butterfly! Butterfly! Butterfly!

(Pinkerton and Sharpless burst into the room, and run to her side. With a weak gesture Butterfly points to her child and dies. Pinkerton kneels down beside her, while Sharpless goes to pick up the child.)

FINE

END

PHOTO CREDITS

Madama Butterfly

GIACOMO PUCCINI

COMPACT DISC ONE   72:07:00

Atto Primo/Act One